CLAIMING EARTH

Other Books by Haki R. Madhubuti

*Black Men: Obsolete, Single, Dangerous? The Afrikan
        American Family in Transition*
Confusion By any Other Name:
        *Essays Exploring the Negative Impact of the
        Blackman's Guide to Understanding the Blackwoman*
From Plan to Planet:
        Life Studies; The Need for Afrikan Minds and Institutions
Enemies: The Clash of Races
A Capsule Course in Black Poetry Writing
        *(co-authored with Gwendolyn Brooks, Keorapetse
        Kgositsile and Dudley Randall)*

Poetry
Killing Memory, Seeking Ancestors
Earthquakes and Sunrise Missions
Book of Life
Directionscore: New and Selected Poems
We Walk the Way of the New World
Don't Cry, Scream
Black Pride
Think Black

Criticism
Dynamite Voices: Black Poets of the 1960's

Anthologies
Why L.A. Happened:
        Implications of the '92 Los Angeles Rebellion
Say That the River Turns:
        The Impact of Gwendolyn Brooks
To Gwen, With Love
        (co-edited with Pat Brown and Francis Ward)

CLAIMING EARTH:

RACE, RAGE, RAPE, REDEMPTION;

Blacks Seeking a Culture of Enlightened Empowerment

HAKI R. MADHUBUTI

THIRD WORLD PRESS • CHICAGO, IL

Claiming Earth: Race, Rage, Rape, Redemption
Blacks Seeking A Culture Of Enlightened Empowerment

Some of these essays have appeared as is or in slightly altered form in *Black Books Bulletin, Catalyst, Too Much Schooling, Too Little Education* (ed. by Mwalimo Shujaa), *A Call to Action* (ed. by Linda M. Thurston), and *Transforming a Rape Culture* (ed. by Buchwald, Fletcher and Roth).

First Edition
First Printing 1995

ISBN: 0-88378-090-9

Library of Congress #: 92-63014

Third World Press
P.O. Box 19730
Chicago, IL 60619

Cover photograph by David Schulz

Cover design by Craig Taylor

Manufactured in the United States of America

94 95 96 97 98 99   10 9 8 7 6 5 4 3 2 1

Dedicated to:

Dr. William Robert Jarrett
(1953—1993)

With an earth-based heart,
he was water and sun to us
and he smiled a lot.

Gwendolyn Brooks
Betty Shabazz   Ossie Davis   Ruby Dee   Avery Brooks

Abena Joan Brown
Barbara Sizemore
John Henrik Clarke
Delores E. Cross
Vivian Gordon

Our Best

and
The Students of Chicago State University
Studying and Struggling to be Our Best.

In memory of

Chancellor Williams
Audre Lorde
Arthur Ashe
Ralph Ellison
Dizzy Gillespie
Alex Haley
John G. Jackson
Charles Gordon Burroughs
Thurgood Marshall
Jacqueline B. Vaughn
Miles Davis
Addison Gayle, Jr.
Darwin T. Turner
Yekini Cynthia Mae Williams

They all brought light
    Helped to change a world
        Enabling us to smile across cultures

Acknowledgements

A book like this requires a great deal of consultation and sleeplessness. I work best in the early mornings (4 a.m. to 11 a.m.). Often, I would call friends, co-workers, and my editor to bounce ideas off them. Without them, this would be a different book and I would still be writing it. Many thanks to Bakari Kitwana, Beverly Guy-Sheftall, Lu Palmer, Vivian Gordon, Useni Eugene Perkins, Helen Spencer, Joyce A. Joyce, and others. It goes without saying that my family—Inez Hall, Laini, Bomani, Akili, Don (Shabaka), and Mari—are to be thanked for giving me the time and space to complete this book. As to most of the ideas contained between these covers, I am indebted to my wife Safisha who challenged me to write what was really on my mind and to go beyond the expected. Love to all. However, I remain responsible for whatever errors that may exist.

H.R.M.

QUESTION

When do we call destruction our own? When do we resist the logic of white supremacy and Black self-hatred? J. D. is a 32 year old Black man who lives with his momma. He does not work and will not take an entry level job because he can do better on the streets. J. D. beat his momma last week for not bringing him cigarettes home. He has six children by five different women and none of them call him daddy. They call him J. D.; he is a small representation of the Black community. Some say the J. D.s and their women are a strong 25 percent. Most of our people are walking tall, working multiple jobs, carrying the weight of family, history, and the current ills and hurts of the 25 percent of J. D.s that increase daily. We can not hide or run from a quarter of our blood and bones. They are here, in need, and dangerous—talk to bus and cab drivers, listen to the children in our schools, talk to mail carriers, policemen, doctors, social workers, barbershop owners, beauticians, and teachers who take self defense classes because they do not teach anymore (many watch their backs and do social work). When do we say No! to misguided teenaged boys and young men who disrespect their elders and whose identity are multiple earrings, beepers, starter jackets, pants low across the cracks of their butts, their initials carved out on the back of their heads, untied sports shoes, four letter words, and faces that never smile in public? They are our sons. They are loaded weapons and most of them have never known the power of love. We have not yet become Haiti or Rwanda, but we are about to go over the cliff blindfolded. We are not the music we used to be. I grew up with the Four Tops, the Dells, the Supremes (before they became Diana Ross and the Supremes), the Miracles, the Temptations, Marvin Gaye, Aretha Franklin, the Intruders, Black love music of self love and Black responsibility. We did not kill each other to gain a street corner or a reputation. When do we call destruction our own?

It is time to come home. This book is a wake-up call and an answer.

CONTENTS

CLAIMING EARTH:
FIGHTING A CULTURE OF CONTAINMENT

Introduction

This is not a "nature" book; however, it is a book about the most precious of natural resources, human beings—specifically Black people in the United States—and our relationship to other people, the earth and its resources. This is very much a political book, somewhat like my other books, but with several important exceptions: I wanted to know who really owns the earth, the planet. I wanted to know why we are here in America, contained in concrete projects for the most part, removed from life-giving, life-determining, life-sustaining, and life-saving elements: land. I wanted to understand the subtleties of modern economic, political, and racial enslavement, and the secrets of cultural, political, economic, and social liberation.

Around the turn of the century, Black people in the United States owned about nineteen million acres of land. Today, Black ownership of land (the only thing that nobody anywhere is making more of) is down to less than three million acres. The African American population is thirty-five million. If that three million acres were divided equally among our people, each person would own .0857 acres of land—not enough for a person to be concerned about, especially if most Blacks think as we have been taught, as individuals, separate, and apart from our community.

This book is not an investigation of the environment; rather, it is about questioning our noninvolvement in the environmentalist movement. Why is it that many urban children think that the source of all food is the corner grocery store or the chain supermarket? It is obvious to any thinking person that part of the health problem in urban areas is closely tied to fast-food restaurants, bad water, the over-consumption of processed foods, the nonavailability of fresh fruits, vegetables, and up-to-date health information. Environmental racism is partially manifested by the toxic dumps, incinerators, and landfills located close to Black communities. It is also about the exploitative use of land and its resources to benefit the few at the deadly expense of the less powerful and less informed.

I also wanted to know why, when it comes to the care and education of Black children, so many of them are at risk in the present-day environment. Why is it that so many of our children are dying so rapidly and so young? It is not that I have not asked these and other questions before (see *Black Men:Obsolete, Single and Dangerous? The African American Family in Transition*). My aim in *Claiming Earth* is to articulate a politics of empowerment at an individual, community, and people level that is intimately tied to educational, economic, social, and environmental development and human politics for the many, rather than the corrupt few.

As I write about culture, I am only continuing my own cultural exploration in a more individualized format, one in which the "me" and "you" are connected to the collective. Therefore, this is not a book about victimization. *Claiming Earth* is about moving from victimhood to self-reliance, to ownership of self, resources, land, and, yes, our tomorrows. I wanted to know why most people on this earth are "dirt" poor. Why is it that most people work from sun-up to sun-down and still do not have enough food for their children? I wanted to know about the less than ten percent of the world's population that is filthy rich and living in obscene wealth. I continue to question why Black people are ignorant of their own identity, which is closely tied to their miseducation, which is also a source of Black powerlessness. I do not come to you as a beggar or as a man crying into the wind, but as an empowered Black man who is a part of a dynamic African (Black) community that is culturally strong and psychologically secure. This community is politically astute and works overtime to make life better for our people. This is a book of hope. For we are a people locked into, engrossed by, and consumed in a political and spiritual history that demands that we rise each day dedicated to making life better and worth living for all people.

Such a history is directly connected to one's quality of life. It is also manifested in seeking the best that the universe has to offer—known and unknown. This history, one that is African in its source, is the life force that fuels and drives the soul in each of us. W. E. B. Du Bois named this force *The Souls of Black Folks*. *Claiming Earth* is a personal work, and I've had to pull on the culture and politics of my teachers, my own history, as well as the work of many who have given great thought to the Black condition.

As I write this, 800,000 Black men and close to 50,000 Black women are imprisoned in this country—more than are imprisoned in any other industrialized country, including South Africa. Why are young Black men dying at such an alarming rate and so often at the hands of each other? And those who escape death are being snatched from our community like sand in a wind storm. Black prisoners in jails across the U. S. are locked up in the most vicious of conditions, most serving lengthy mandatory sentences. Once inside, they fight to survive while being trained to be real criminals. Many of these men will be released back to their communities with a mindset of double self-hatred, only to end up back in prison after unleashing untold harm on their own people.

I also question the current condition and the quality of Black male-female relationships, or, as I call the ones that work, loveships. My inquiry is always toward understanding strategies for making these relationships better. How do we reverse the destruction within? I still believe that many of our problems begin in unhealthy families and fractured personal associations that could be avoided with a little bit of cultural knowledge and a lot more commitment.

Finally, I am always in search of healthy rituals that aid our continued renewal. It is a universal fact that individuals must take control of their own mental and physical health upon entering adulthood. Bad habits must be discarded; new ways of thinking, experiencing life, eating, exercising, relaxing, entertaining, cleansing (internal and external), and maintaining and developing friendships and loveships must be considered. How does one deal with the negative effects of a highly white supremacist, politically and economically corrupt culture without losing one's own sense of beauty and harmony while functioning in a culture one wishes to change?

There are clear and thoughtful answers to all of these concerns. Our history, contemporary and ancient, is one that does not have to take a back seat to any people. Having listened to and learned from the best of our cultural thinkers—Chancellor Williams, John Henrik Clarke, Cheikh Anta Diop, Harold Cruse, Bobby Wright, Barbara Sizemore, John G. Jackson, Gwendolyn Brooks, Malcolm X, Wade Nobles, Hoyt W. Fuller, Frances Cress Welsing, and literally hundreds of others—I am convinced that we have the intellectual foundation, spiritual/moral mandate, and vision among us to transform our society as well as the world.

The solutions offered in this book are not the last answers. Many other solutions have been and will be published by writers often more insightful and intelligent than I. But few love African (Black) people and all children more than I. And, for me, there is something about white supremacy and power, money and greed, politics and governing, land and ownership, agriculture and production, education and self-concepts, addiction and control, attitudes and love, dependency and powerlessness that is missing in the very large equation of the Black condition that keeps sending me back to the question I started with: Who owns the earth?

Most certainly not the people.
not the hands that work the waterways,
nor the backs bending in the sun,
or the bony fingers soldering transistors,
not the legs walking the massive fields,
or the knees glued to the pews of storefronts or granite churches
not the bloated bellies on toothpick legs.
All victims of decisions
made at the Washington Monument and Lenin's tomb
by aged actors viewing
red dawn and the return of rambo part ix.

CULTURE AND RACE

Race, Rage and Intellectual Development

A Personal Journey

This is not fiction, nor is it complete autobiography. I share this slice of my life only to make a connection to readers that may indeed be impossible to make in any other way. I do not believe in victimology, even though I am a victim. As an intelligent, productive Black man, husband, father, poet, teacher, publisher, editor, community cultural worker, political entrepreneur, and "brother," my story, with all its horror and unforgettable heart-breaking insights, is not unusual in the context of growing up in Urban America. However, in the final (and hopefully most revealing) analysis, self-examination, self-realization, and self-definition in the context of a known and understood history are the first steps toward enlightened empowerment.

If I extend my hand as a willing victim of American racism (white supremacy) and leave it at that, I do you—the reader—no good and ultimately fail myself. It is easy, yet debilitating and weakening, to be a victim. Being a victim, living as the object of victimization, is the denial of the possibility to become more than others (who don't like you or your family) think you can become. A victim is not a contributor; rather, he or she is but a child-like participant, looking for the easy and less difficult or responsible way to survive. Victimhood is modern enslavement with invisible, reinforced steel chains firmly placed around one's legs, arms, and mind. Anytime you capture a person's mind, nine times out of ten, you have his or her body as well. Victimhood is the prerequisite to self-hatred and dependency, political and economic neutralization and joyless living. I ask myself two questions every day: (1) What good can I do for myself, my family, my extended family, Black people, and others today? (2) How can I continue to rise above the limiting expectations of others, especially my enemies?

I now share these factual slices from my life only to place myself in a cultural and historical context.

I grew up on the Lower East Side of Detroit and West Side of Chicago in a family that lived too often from week to week. My mother, sister, and I represented the nucleus of our family. In 1943, my mother, migrated from Little Rock, Arkansas, moving, as John O. Killens would say, 'up-South' to Michigan. She came with my father, who stayed long enough to father my sister, who is a year-and-a-half younger than I. I was born in 1942.

Those years, the 1940s and 1950s, were not kind to us, and my father wandered in and out of our lives from the day we hit Detroit. My mother, alone with two children and no skills, ended up working as a janitor in an apartment building owned by a Negro preacher/undertaker. My earliest memory is of her cleaning that three-story, sixteen-unit building each day, carrying garbage cans on her back to the alley once a week. Seldom did I see her without a broom, mop, or wash cloth in her hands. By this time, I was eight years old, and my sister was seven. We helped as much as possible because we knew that staying in our basement apartment depended upon our keeping the building clean. I did not know then that our housing also depended upon my mother's sexual involvement with the Negro building owner. These encounters took place when we were at school or while we were asleep. My mother began to trade her body quite early in order for us to live. In the 1950s, there were few safety nets for single women with children. Consequently, my mother became a victim in a white supremacist, monied system, which allowed some Black men to become surrogate oppressors.

With no family in Detroit and left to her own limited resources, my mother sought to survive with her children in a way that would have the least possible negative impact on us. However, due to the violent nature of her relationship with the landlord, we stayed in our Lower East Side apartment only until she was able to find work less threatening and taxing on her physically and psychologically. At least that is what my sister and I thought. What I've failed to tell you about my mother is that she was probably one of the most beautiful women in the world. I've seen her beauty not only stop traffic but compel men to literally get out of their cars to introduce themselves to her. Her beauty, which was both physical and internal, was something that the few women she associated with could handle. Women would stare at her with dropped mouths. Her beauty would ultimately place her in an environment that would destroy her.

My mother's next job was that of a barmaid. She started serving drinks at one of the newest and classiest locations in Detroit, Sonny Wilson's. Along with this job came the slow but destructive habit of alcohol consumption. Also, she began to run in very fast company. She was named Miss Barmaid of 1951, carrying with that title all of the superficiality and glitter of the Negro entertainment world at that time. To cut to the bone of all of this is to note rather emphatically that my family's condition of poverty drove my mother into a culture that dictated both her destruction and great misery for my sister and me. By the time I was thirteen, my mother was a confirmed alcoholic and was fast losing her health. When I turned fifteen, she had moved to hard drugs and was not functional most of the time.

My sister, who had just turned fourteen, announced to us that she was pregnant. This was in the late 1950s and pregnancy out of wedlock was not a common or acceptable occurrence. I went looking for the man who had impregnated her. He was a local gang leader, twenty-one years old, who had as much potential as a husband or father as I did at fifteen. After briefly talking to him about my sister's condition and getting virtually nowhere, I did what most "men" did in similar situations at that time: I hit him. And he, in a rather surgical fashion, responded by literally "kicking my ass." After reporting this to my mother, she, in a drunken stupor, gave me another whipping for getting whipped.

Shortly after that incident, my mother's need for alcohol and drugs increased. She prostituted herself to feed her habit. Many nights I searched Detroit's transient hotels looking for her. Needless to say, I had grown up rather quickly and felt that there was no hope for me or my sister. Just before I turned sixteen, my mother overdosed on drugs and died. She had been physically and sexually abused by someone so badly that we were not able to view her body at her funeral. My sister was pregnant again. By the time she was twenty, she had three children. Before she was thirty, she had six children and had never been married. She has endured a life of pain and difficulty that often has been the exact duplicate of our mother's. To this day she lives in great pain.

I could not cry at my mother's funeral. My heart was cold and my mind was psychologically tired. I felt a quiet feeling of relief and release at her death, but also an underlying tone of guilt. At sixteen, I felt that I had not done enough to save my mother. However, it was clear to me that her final days had been filled with long hours of tragic suffering over which she had no control. All I could do was watch in confused pain, hostility, anger, resentment, and rage.

At first, I could not understand my anger. Why did she have to die so young and so viciously? Why were my sister, her baby, and I alone without help or hope? Why were we so poor? It seemed that my life was one big fight. There was no escape from problems and very little peace. And I guess my mother's death brought a moment of peace. The fight to survive remained uppermost in my mind. Yet it seemed I was being torn apart from the inside. A part of my own fear was connected to how my sister and I were going to survive. I had seen and been a part of too much destruction and death in my young life. I knew that the only person who really cared about our future was me, and that was not enough.

I had few friends, partially because of my economic condition; I had little time to play because I had to work. Also, my social skills were not the best and the path of the loner best suited me at that time. I did not realize then that my solitary existence was to eventually save my life.

Color in America

A part of the problem that my mother, sister, and I faced

in America was that our skin color was neither Black nor white, but yellow! The unusual beauty that centered in my mother was not only due to the distinctive bone structure of her face and her small, well-connected body. It also had to do with the fact that all of her physical beauty was wrapped in yellow. Yes, we were Arkansas Blacks, but my mother could easily have passed for Puerto Rican or dark Italian if she did not have to open her mouth. Her language was Southern Black English, and it carried in it the rural slowness that urban America does not have pity on.

However, it was her beauty, illuminated by very light skin color that attracted the darkest of Black men and, of those I remember, the most abusive of Black men. They seemed to be steaming in anger, hatred, and internal rage. It seems as though by being with her, they were as close to white women as was allowed at that time. And their often intense love/hate relationship with her was only a mirror of the fight they were having daily with themselves and the white world. They could not touch or physically retaliate against white people, but my mother was there for many of them to play out their deepest hurt in their "loving" and abusive treatment of her. I was not to understand, until much later, the deep color-rage that plagued them and that lay at the surface of my own reality.

Being a "yellow nigger" in urban America was like walking on roasted toothpicks hanging from the mouths of brothers who did not like the taste of wood or understand themselves. Many of the Black men who populated my early life used self-defacing language twenty-four hours a day. The two operative words used constantly were "nigger" and "mothafucka." We had not only been seasoned to dislike or hate the "us" in us, but also had adopted the language of self-abuse and self-hatred. I learned early to walk the fine line between Black and white. I began to understand the anger, hatred, and rage in me by studying Black literature and Black music.

What Saved Me?

At thirteen, my mother asked me to go to the Detroit Public Library to check out a book for her. The title of the book was *Black Boy* by Richard Wright. I refused to go because I didn't want to go anywhere asking for anything Black. The self-hatred that occupied my mind, body, and soul simply prohibited me from going to a white library in 1955 to request from a white librarian a book by a Black author, especially with "Black" in the title.

I and millions of other young Blacks were products of a white educational system that at best taught us to read and respect the literary, creative, scientific, technological, and commercial development of others. No one actually told me, "you should hate yourself." However, the images, symbols, products, creations, promotions, and authorities of white America all very subtlety and often quite openly taught me white supremacy, taught me to hate myself.

This white supremacist philosophy of life was unconsciously reinforced in Black homes, churches, clubs, schools, and communities throughout the nation. Therefore, my refusal to go check out *Black Boy* was only in keeping with a culture that twenty-four hours a day not only denied me and my people fundamental rights and privileges as citizens, but refused to admit that we were whole human beings. Few articulated it in popular culture at that time, but we lived in Apartheid, U.S.A.

However, *Black Boy* had somehow attached itself to my mother's mind and would not let go. I went to the library, found the book on the shelf myself, put it to my chest, found an unpeopled spot, and began to read the book that would profoundly alter my life.

For the first time in my life, I was reading words developed into ideas that were not insulting to my own personhood. Richard Wright's experiences were mine even though we were separated by geography. I read close to half of the book before the library closed. I checked *Black Boy* out, hurried home, went into the room I shared with my sister, and read for the rest of the night. Upon completing *Black Boy* the next morning, I was somehow a different type of questioner in school and at home. I had not totally changed, but the foundation had been planted. Deeply. I became more concerned about the shape of things around me. I also read Wright's *Native Son, Uncle Tom's Cabin,* and *12 Million Black Voices.* Richard Wright painted pictures with words that connected to the real me. I could relate to Bigger Thomas because his fears, doubts, and internal rage were the same that I experienced. Layers of ignorance were being removed by just opening my mind to a world that included me as a whole person. Wright entered my life at the right time.

After my mother's death, I took the Greyhound to Chicago, where I stayed with an aunt for a while, then I rented a room at the Southside YMCA. I completed high school in Chicago and ended up in St. Louis, Missouri, where I joined the United States Army.

The military was the poor boy's employment. On the way to basic training at Fort Leonard Wood, Missouri, I was reading

Paul Robeson's *Here I Stand*. When we arrived at boot camp, the white, middle-thirtyish drill sergeant ordered us off the bus. We were about two hundred men. Three Black men, including myself, and one hundred ninety-seven white men. The Black men had all joined voluntarily, but most of the white men were drafted. This was 1960, and the Army was practicing "integration."

As I stepped off the bus, the white drill sergeant sighted Paul Robeson's face on my book and snatched it from my hand. He pulled me out of line and barked into my face, "what's your Negro mind doing reading this Black communist?" Of course, many thoughts ran through my head as potential responses to his question. This was the first time I had heard a double negative used so creatively. The drill sergeant ordered all of us up against the bus and commenced to tear the pages from the book, giving a page to each recruit, and telling the recruits to use the pages for toilet paper. By this time, I was questioning my own sanity about joining the military and examining my options.

Luckily, I was also reading John O. Killens' *And Then We Heard the Thunder*, a powerful and telling book about Black men in Europe's War on the World Number Two (commonly referred to as World War II). What I learned from Killens was the importance of using one's time wisely and never to speak from the top of one's head in anger when outnumbered. As I stood, lips closed, cold and shaking with fear, anger, and loneliness—while the sergeant destroyed my copy of Robeson's work—I decided four things that would stay with me for the rest of my life:

1.   I would never, never again apologize for being Black. I am

who I am, I realized then, and if Black literature has taught me anything, it clarified for me that I was a man of African descent in America serving time in the United States Army rather than the United Sates prison system.

2. I would never again put myself in a cultural or intellectual setting where people outside of my culture or race would know more about me than I knew about myself. This meant that I had to go on the offense and put myself on a re-education program that prepared me internally as an African in America, as a Black man.

3. I was in the United States Army because I was Black, poor, and ignorant of the forces that controlled my life and the lives of other men—Black and white—with whom I was to train. These forces were racial, economic and political, and I needed accurate information on all of them. While many of the other brothers in my platoon searched for fun, I visited the libraries. Few could understand why I chose to be alone with books. The reason was that I found new friends, uncritical friends in the literature. I was a sponge. Reading became as important as water and food.

4. If *ideas* were that powerful and could cause such a reaction, then I was going to get into the *idea* business. For that drill sergeant to act so violently against a book that contained ideas that he probably did not even understand was frightening. He was reacting to the image and idea of Paul Robeson that had been created by monied, political, and mass media white power brokers.

From that day on, I have been on a mission to understand the world and to be among the progressive men who want to change it for the benefit of the majority who occupy it.

My two years and ten months in the military was essentially my undergraduate education. I read close to a book a day, concentrating in history, political science, Black literature, and (of course) Black poetry—the written/oral music of our people. I read and re-read, studied the history and culture of Black people, and extended my study into the areas of political economy. One of the most influential writers to impact my thinking was W. E. B. Du Bois.

Du Bois had already articulated that the problem of the twentieth century would be color. As I studied his work, I began to see possibilities for myself for two reasons: (1) Du Bois was a high-yellow Black man who had devoted his life to the uncompromising development and liberation of Black people; and (2) his writing represented liberating medicine for my mind. All of Du Bois' work whether in sociology, politics, fiction, or poetry led to the reconstruction of the Black mind. The passage that both freed me intellectually and gave meaning to the rage that continued to tear me apart came from *The Souls of Black Folk*:

> After the Egyptian and the Indian, the Greek and Roman, the Teuton and Mongolian, the Negro is a sort of seventh son, born with a veil and gifted with second sight in this American world—a world which yields him no true self-consciousness, but only lets him see himself through the revelation of the other world. It is a peculiar sensation, this double consciousness, this sense of always looking at one's self through the eyes of others, of measuring one's soul by the tape of a world that looks on in amused contempt and pity.
>
> One ever feels his twoness—an American, a Negro; two souls, two thoughts, two unreconciled strivings; two warring ideals in one dark body, whose dogged strength alone keeps it form being torn asunder. The history of the American Negro is the history of this strife—this longing to attain self-

conscious manhood to merge his double self into a better and
truer self.

Yes, I knew that I was different and Black. However, it
was Du Bois' analysis that brought me to where I could
appreciate and begin to reconcile the different "selves" in me.
Color and psychology, color and history, color and enslavement, color and politics, color and economics, color and rage,
took on new meanings for me. I came to understand that the
white images and symbols that assigned me to certain roles in
life had nothing to do with the quality and content of my history
or my mind. My search for authenticity was being led by the
literature of W. E. B. Du Bois and others.

However, Du Bois' *Black Reconstruction* and *The World
and Africa* were the two books that ultimately unlocked my
brain and liberated my own thought. Dr. Du Bois was a Black
intellectual who remained true to his calling in that he not only
wrote and documented history, he, by his actions, via the
NAACP (National Association for the Advancement of Colored People) and other progressive organizations, tried to
change the world for the best. He went to his grave in Ghana
in 1963 at the age of ninety-five, never giving in to the "long and
comfortable compromises." Du Bois was a political activist for
life.

I left the military in August 1963. In September of that
same year, four little girls were murdered in Birmingham,
Alabama. They were bombed in their church while praying to
a God who did not even look like them. This violent act against
our children confirmed for me the course of my life. For two
years and ten months, I had been trained to be a killer in the U.S.
Army. Later, I realized that all the targets I shot at were either

Black or colored. However, I also knew then the color of the people who were blowing up our children. To this day, they, and the millions of brain mismanaged Negroes that they control, continue to tap-dance on the dreams of our children.

I am against dancing to and entertaining the enemies of the world. As a young man, I re-educated myself. The poet-writer that I've become is directly connected to my education and political involvement over the last thirty-four years. Each day, I also realize that I, too, am an activist for life and that serious struggle and organizing will only bear fruit if it is ongoing, institutionalized, rethought, updated, involves the young, remains honest, and is open-minded and combative. Struggle must be renewing and productive if it is to grow. Additionally, one must struggle with like-minded people.

The rage that I and most sane people feel toward the death and human damage inflicted upon the weak by this society and others must be channeled and released in a healthy manner. Otherwise, we internalize it or let it loose on those persons closest to us.

Often our lives may seem like pieces of slave fiction; however, by seriously studying history and political economy, we can come to understand that one way we can have an impact on the nightmare that covers the lives of most people is through organized struggle at every level of human involvement. If such cultural work is to be fruitful, we must concentrate on that which we are *for* as opposed to only fighting and articulating that which we are *against*.

This is not rhetoric or "playground" boasting. If the condition of our people and that of the majority of the world's people is not proof enough of the destructive path we are on, we are truly lost. Our greatest tasks remain (1) discovering a way to neutralize racism and oppression without becoming racists and oppressors ourselves, (2) destroying an abusive economic system while trying to create something better, (3) reversing destructive habits with the knowledge of that which is best and better? We cannot build on the anti only. I am African. I am Black (a political, cultural, and color designation in the U.S.), even though my skin complexion is what is loosely described as high yellow. Yet, to look at me any time of the day or night few would conclude that I am any person other than one of African descent. I am clear about this fact just as I am certain that all Black people descended from the continent of Africa. That this is still debatable in some quarters speaks highly of the global effects of white world supremacy propaganda (see Frances Cress Welsing's *The Isis Papers: The Keys to the Colors*, John Henrik Clarke's *Notes For An African World Revolution*, Marimba Ani's *Yurugu: An African-centered Critique of European Cultural Thought and Behavior* and Chancellor Williams' *The Destruction of Black Civilization*).

I have travelled to Africa at least eight times. I am not sure because I stopped counting after I realized that my journeys were more about me centering myself, rather than going to give papers, participate in international gatherings, or to read my poetry. Africa had become source, a connecting spirit that revitalized me, a place where I could gather new knowledge and the best cure for Africa romanticism.

Again, it was the literature that pointed me to Africa—Du Bois yes, but also Carter G. Woodson, Alaine Locke, Langston Hughes, Marcus Garvey and, Richard Wright (especially his 1954 book on Ghana and Kwame Nkrumah, *Black Power*). My life changed as the knowledge I absorbed lifted me into the African world community of builders, creators, inventors, and producers. Reading, studying, reflecting and internalizing the words and works of Black (African) authors represented a type of cultural food that would shape me into the culturally conscious man that I am today. Ideas about the African (Black) reality became liberating food. I consumed Black (African) ideas and literature like a desert taking to raindrops. I learned to stop making excuses for Black people as well as for whites. It should be a given fact that everything Black is not right. There are many good white people in the world—the problem is that they are in the minority and do not hold power.

There is no separation between my cultural self and my political, professional, business, familial, and writer selves. I am one, and I am clear—always open for new knowledge, ideas, and revelations, but firmly anchored and connected to the millions of African (Black) women and men that led the way for my enlightenment and normalcy. Those of us that understand this must be at the forefront of creating, producing, and building that which we are for and sharing such development with our families, extended families, community, and world. It is easy to be against any number of ideas and institutions. The larger task is to fight that which we consider evil and build that which we consider good, just, and correct.

The role of the Black intellectual is not only to understand the text, but to write his/her version of the story, to teach the young the positive objectives of life, but to be involved at a community level—where theory is often never tested—in making real and substantive, long-term change in the lives of those who are truly suffering.

This is transforming work. It is moral and ethical work. The monetary rewards are few, if any. However, the love generated by the hope in the eyes of our children as a result of such work is for me the best payment. We must give our children a fighting chance in a world that long ago counted them out, diminished their chances of success to below zero. To see the yeses in their eyes is also to hear the yeses in our own heartbeats. This is why the drum is our magical instrument: you cannot kill the beat of hungry hearts.

CULTURE

The culture of a people is their definition.

The African/Black in us is the water, earth, air, fire, and wind forming the core that produces the fuel energizing the spirits and souls that center our creation.

The sum total of a peoples' existence is exhibited in their culture, from the food grown, prepared and consumed to the clothes they make and wear, the god(s) they worship and the spirit manifested as a result of that worship, the music calling the drum in them producing the dance that glues them together in sharing movement and oneness, the visual art that replicates their souls and ideas for the others and themselves to see, the words—oral and written—marking their existence that form the history and heritage of each moment catching all new creations in fiction and non-fiction, poetry disguised as song and drama in melodies that move the feet of the bodies toward the transportation that carries them throughout the planet especially among their own villages, towns and cities that ultimately harnesses the depth, the beauty, the ugliness, the technically unusable, the happiness, the magnificence, the rottenness, the kindness, the love, the rough-rawness, the refined carefulness, the unusual thoughtfulness, the occasional queerness, the quiet unexpectedness, an economy of fairness, the ripe laughter, the largeness and smallness of our souls, to the war and peace in each of us: confirming culture.

The culture of a people represents life, source, soul, spirit, saneness, silliness, science, smiles, seriousness and connected-ness: family.

This familyhood confirms and confirms
in an undying love that is burned into the souls of each newborn
binding them biologically and culturally
to life, source, spirit saneness, smiles, seriousness and memory
        that
                passes on immortality,
                passes on the heartbeats of genius,
                passes on respect for others,
                passes on earthgrown love,
                passes on the permanence of family,
community, nation, people, culminating in the unique
        celebration of themselves.
spirited community.

This is culture. replicate.

CULTURAL WORK

Planting New Trees with New Seeds

I n America, people of African descent are caught between a hurricane and a volcano when it comes to the acquisition of life-giving and life-sustaining knowledge. Too many of our children are trapped in urban school systems that have been "programmed" for failure. All too often, the answer to what must be done to correct this injustice is left in the hands of those most responsible for creating the problem. If your child is sleeping and a rat starts to bite at his/her head you don't ask the rat to please stop biting at your child's brain. If you are a sane, normal, and loving parent, you go on the attack and try your damnedest to kill the rat.

When it comes to the education of African American children, rats are biting at the doors, floors, desks, and gym shoes of the nation's public schools. Jonathan Kozol, in his heartfelt book *Savage Inequalities* (1993), documents the near collapse of urban public education. He writes of young people who "have no feeling of belonging to America." If public education is the first formal, state-sponsored orientation into becoming a productive citizen, the country is in deep, deep trouble. If public schooling is supposed to stimulate the nation's children into becoming poets, doctors, teachers, scientists, farmers, computer experts, musicians, entrepreneurs, carpenters, professors, etc., get ready to throw in the towel. This is the eleventh round and the major answer that is offered by most urban school systems is simply to change the superintendent. Rather than look at the system, we personalize the problem as if one man or woman can affect real change. For example, in a city like Chicago where sixty years of "boss" politics control a $2.7 billion school budget, change and child-centered education takes a back seat to economics and patronage. To bring an "unschooled" outsider in as superintendent is like a chicken prescribing chicken soup for a cold.

Why is it that in 1994 we still lie to ourselves? Some of the most intelligent advocates of public school education continue to blame the victim as if our children have the capacity to educate themselves. They overlook the ever-present political, racial, and economic realities of the major consumers of public education: Black and Latino children. They overlook the all-consuming cultures of defeat and poverty that blanket large portions of the Black community. The metaphorical "rat" I speak of is white supremacy (racism), which manifests itself freely in the structured and systematic destruction of millions of unsuspecting children and their parents.

It is argued in some quarters in the Black community that a public school education can be a handicap to one's survival. Young brothers seen too often with books (without pictures) are categorized as unmanly. However, this view is unenlightened and represents a small slice of the miseducation that is accepted and encouraged by a growing number of people with enslaved minds enclosed in short-circuited memories. On the other hand, white supremacist ideology has a way of making another type of enslaved mind think that by acquiring pieces of paper (degrees) he/she is indeed free. Yet, the one freedom that is openly accessible to all Black folks in America is the freedom to self-destruct.

Memory is instructive here. Africans did not swim, motor boat, or free fly to America. There is a horrible connection between Africans and Europeans that must not be forgotten, negated, or minimized. The African holocaust is seldom explored or taught in our schools. This relationship of white slave trader to enslaved African has been the glue connecting us for over a millennium.

There are over 100 million people of African descent in the Western hemisphere, and we all face similar problems. Whether one is in Canada, the United States, or Brazil, the fight for self-definition and self-reliance is like using a shovel to dig a hole in steel-enforced concrete. There are over 69 million people of African descent in Brazil who speak Portuguese, there are over 35 million people of African descent in the U.S. who attempt to speak English, and we Africans don't talk to each other. I maintain that this is a learned activity and acutely cultural. Over one hundred million Africans moving and working for the same goals in the same hemisphere is a threat to anyone's rule. Our clothes, names, street address, employment, and articulations in their languages have changed, but the basic relationship has remained the same: Black folks are still dependent upon white folks in America. To Africanize or to liberate this system from its exclusive Euro-American model is indeed a progressive and often revolutionary act.

Another memory. I'll never forget a trip I made to Tanzania in the 1970s to attend an international conference. After the day's work, I walked alone in the city. As the sun set and the street lights illuminated the city of Dar es Salaam, I noticed three children about a block away huddled close together under a lamp post. As I approached them, I noticed that my presence was not important to them. I smiled at the reason why. The three of them, two boys and a girl, were deeply engrossed in reading and discussing a book. I walked on without disturbing them in their obvious joy. These were poor African children using the only light available at that time. Their enthusiasm for learning was at one time the reality for the great majority of African Americans.

The history of the fight to educate African Americans is one that is rarely told in this age of integration. In fact, if the truth was ever unshackled, it would reveal that students in Black schools along with Black church members led the modern fight for full educational and political equality in the U.S. This fight was never a battle to sit next to white children in a classroom. It was and still is a struggle for an equal and level playing field in all areas of human endeavor: finance, law, politics, military, commerce, sports, entertainment, science, technology, and education.

Many believed that if we had first rate facilities, buildings, supplies, environment, teachers, and support personnel, a quality education would follow. This is obviously not true. We now understand that there is a profound difference between going to school and being educated. We know that close to a half-million children frequent the Chicago Public Schools each day and less than twenty percent are truly receiving a first-class education that could stand remotely close to that offered by the best private schools.

For the last twenty-five years, I have been involved in the

Independent Black School Movement. This movement grew out of the Black empowerment struggles and initiatives of the 1960s and has developed African-centered schools around the country. It also has established a national professional organization, the Council of Independent Black Institutes (CIBI). The great majority of persons involved in the first generation of this movement were products of the public school system. We knew first hand the type of school not needed. From the beginning, we were (and continue to be) cultural workers who had been tremendously influenced by Black struggle and the works of W. E. B. Du Bois, Carter G. Woodson, Frantz Fanon, Paulo Freire, Marcus Garvey, Harold Cruse, Chancellor Williams, E. Franklin Frazier, Mary McLeod Bethune, and others.

The critical examination of schools and education always has been central in our analysis. The development of our school in Chicago, New Concept Development Center (NCDC), has indeed been a labor of love. Also, I can assure you that it has been a love of that type of labor. Because if the love was not there, we would not have a school. Our 23 years of developing NCDC have been extremely difficult and have taxed us both physically and emotionally. The question of schools vs. education is not a question of becoming an "educated fool"; the fear of book learning disconnecting one from community development has a long tradition in the Black community. In fact, in our community a distinction has always been made between schools and education. Since we had to fight so hard to get a foot into the schoolhouse door, the struggle to go to school has, in itself, meant to most Africans in America that a quality education would not necessarily be the results of such an endeavor.

James D. Anderson, in his brilliant book, *The Education of Blacks in the South 1860-1935*, makes it clear that Africans in America viewed education as a birth right in the same light as freedom. The first two types of institutions that Africans built from the ground up with their own hands and resources were schools and churches. Therefore, our continued inquiry into the state of Black education must be an insightful and informed one. Such an examination must be one that asks the difficult questions:

1. What is more important than the enlightened education of our children? Should one's children have any obligation to their own people and culture? Who is ultimately responsible for providing education: the family, the state, or others?

2. Education in the past has been used politically against the advancement of African Americans. Is it any different today? Will African-centered studies connect education to the political, scientific, economic, and racial realities of today's world?

3. The European-American centeredness or Western focus of today's education continues to place conscious Blacks on a collision course with its basic premise: that European culture stands at the center and is pivotal to one's understanding of the world. Is European culture universal? Will the introduction of African-centered thought and pedagogy broaden our students' minds or pigeonhole them into a false sense of security and narrow nationalism? Is African-centered studies a new form of ethnocentrism or exclusivity masked in new terminology and contexts?

4. All education is value-based. Whose values are our children learning? Will African-centered studies teach a value-base that will encourage and allow competition at a world level and cooperation at a local one?

An educated Black person must not only be aware of the core curriculum of his or her school but must also have a core understanding of his/her own peoples' contributions to local, national, and world civilization. When we argue for an African-centered education, it is not at the expense or exclusion of an enlightened Western education; rather, it is an important addition to this knowledge base. Dr. Wade Nobles and his staff have instituted an African-centered curriculum at the McClymonds International Science, Culture and Technology High School in Oakland, California. His program defines African-centered education in the following ways:

> "Afrocentric, Africentric, or African Centered" are interchangeable terms representing the concept which categorizing a quality of thought and practice which is rooted in the cultural image and interest of people of African ancestry and which represents and reflects the life experiences, history and traditions of people of African ancestry as the center of analyses. Afrocentricity is therein the intellectual and philosophical foundations upon which people of African ancestry should create their own scientific and moral criterion for authenticating the reality of African human processes. It represents the core and fundamental quality of the "Belonging" of people of African ancestry.

> In terms of education, African centered education utilizes African and African American cultural precepts, processes, laws and experiences to solve, guide and understand human functioning relative to the educational process. In essence, Afrocentricity represents the fact that as human beings, people of African ancestry have the right and responsibility to "center" themselves in their own subjective possibilities and potential and through the recentering process reproduce and refine the best of themselves.

We must never lose sight of the fact that Black people in America must function and excel in the cultures in which they live. This means essentially that we must tackle, absorb, decipher, reject, and appreciate European American culture in all of its racism, complexity, contributions, liberating ideas, and models. However, if one is to become and remain a culturally whole African (Black) person, he or she must be first and foremost concerned about the culture of his or her people. To again quote Dr. Nobles:

> African Centered multicultural education is driven by truth, respect for knowledge, desire to learn and a passion for excellence. In regards to "centric" education, the impor- tance of culture is not simply relegated or minimized to the task of being sensitive to cultural differences or superficially appreciating or exploring the common ground of different people. As the foundation for multi-cultural education, culture, as both the process and the subject of education, will serve as the medium and mechanism for teaching, learning, counseling and educational management/administration.

The logic behind this is that in most cases a person's contribu- tion to society is closely related to his or her understanding and perception of himself or herself in relation to the culture in which he or she functions and lives. Such a culture can be one that either enslaves and shortens life or that liberates and gives life. The best protection for any people can be found in culture that is intellectually and psychologically liberating. We should be about the development of whole persons, and should begin that wholeness with an accurate understanding and assessment of our own involvement in our community, city, state, nation, and world.

For example, the normalization of Malcolm X, psycho- logically and intellectually, came about when he was a young man locked up in prison. I say that Malcolm X was normalized rather than radicalized because he was introduced to ideas that challenged and liberated his mind. Ideas that put his people close to the center of civilization. He saw in the teachings of Elijah Muhammad and others a self-protective shield as well as the core wisdom for the making of a new Black person in America. From that point on, Malcolm X prepared himself to go on the offensive, to be proactive and combative in a self-reliant and self-protective manner. Any person, from any culture, functioning *sanely* would have acted the same way.

My own development, or should I say misdevelopment, was not unlike that of millions of Black people in America. I was born into acute poverty, educated in public schools by insensitive and uncaring teachers, and dependent upon a welfare system that was demeaning, inadequate, and corrupt. I was nurtured in a single-parent family where my mother was ill-equipped to navigate the economic, social, and political pressures of our world. All of this drove her to alcohol, drugs, and death at the age of thirty six. My own transformation came about as a direct result of being introduced to African (Black) ideas that did not insult my own personhood, but guided me, invigorated me, and lifted me beyond the white supremacist theories that confined me and my people to the toilets of other people's promises and progress.

All education must lead to deep understanding and mastery. The crucial question is, deep understanding and mastery of what? Introduction to many forms of knowing is absolutely necessary. However, most of the understandings about life that are being taught to our children have ceased to be life-giving and life-sustaining, and do not lend themselves to self-reliance or deep reflection on the state of one's self and one's people in a highly charged, competitive, and often oppressive world. One must be anchored in one's self, people, history, i.e. culture, before one can truly be a whole participant in world culture or multi-culturalism; we must always start local in order to appreciate and incorporate the positive agents of the universal. One cannot achieve the multi-anything if one has not explored the singular inside one first.

African-centered cultural studies must lead, encourage, and direct African American students into the technologies of the future. This is where the new statements about power, control, and wealth are being made in the world today.

Black students must have deep understandings of the political, racial, economic, scientific, and technological realities that confront the very survival of African people locally, nationally, and internationally. They must be grounded in a worldview that promotes cross-cultural communication, understanding, and sharing; yet they must be self-protective enough to realize that the world is not fair and that one's own interests often come into conflict with the interests of others, especially when race is involved. Therefore, if we want our children to achieve significantly, they must adhere to the following:

1. Possess a deep understanding of the world in which they will have to function. However, the foundation of their knowledge must be anchored in positive self-concept and taught in an environment that encourages growth. If one is secure in one's self, that which others project—in all areas—will be less appealing, confusing or threatening.

2. Realize that all education is foundational. The values we practice are introduced early and often in school and non-school settings such as family, media, church, entertainment, sports functions, etc., and can either work for or against development.

3. Understand that successful development is difficult with a quality education, but almost impossible without one. Further, education can be fun, but it is often hard and boring work and requires a commitment far beyond picking up a basketball or learning a new dance or handshake. It demands deep study and quiet time.

4. Understand that multiculturalism, if it is to mean anything, must exist among enlightened cultures who bring their best to the table for discussion. If all people of African descent have to contribute is that from Europe, what does that say about us? How are we any different—in cultural substance—from the ethnic groups of Europe and the United States?

Too Much Schooling, Too Little Education, edited by M. Mwalimi Shujaa, and Useni Eugene Perkins' *Harvesting New Generations* are must reading if we are to completely understand the urgency of this task. Other critical works to study and absorb are Janice Hale-Benson's *Black Children: Their Roots, Culture and Learning Styles,* Nsenga Warfield Coppock's *Transformation: A Rites of Passage Manual for African American Girls*, Carter G. Woodson's *The Miseducation of the Negro*, Amos Wilson's *The Developmental Psychology of the Black Child*, and Wade Nobles' *Africanity and the Black Family*.

Our children are our priority and the only thing more important than their care is the care of ourselves—their parents and teachers—in a way that does not diminish our ability to provide them with the best education in all the life-giving and life-saving areas. To do less is a profound comment on our own cultural education.

LANGUAGE

Is There a Black Way and Does It Matter?

That which is most unique about us, other than the infinite variety of our facial expressions and skin shading, is the musical quality of our utterances. We speak in magical voices. Whether we are from

Harlem or Senegal,

Nigeria or Detroit,

Los Angeles or Kenya,

Jamaica or London,

Rio de Janeiro or Panama.

We bring to language its beat, its cadences, its walking rhythms, its stops and goes, its skips and its balances; we add style and substance to whatever language we communicate, dance, or sing in. There is an African or Black side of most languages. Language is cultural. Our language is our name.

Blacks in America, specifically North America, USA, sing or speak an African American or Black English. The musical quality of Black voices helps to define the regions of the country that one is reared in. Our voices carry our villages. There is a Northern, Southern and Western voice. There are Mississippi, New York, Cleveland, St. Louis, and San Francisco sounds radiating from the Black side of life. Our language carries our history. It is memories being vocalized. All cultures, all people have this. Blacks in this country have been negatively categorized, stigmatized, and put down by others, mainly whites, who are ignorant about the value and beauty of cultural and linguistic differences. The blues is our language; it is our indigenous fiction, short stories that swing.

Black vocal harmonies have influenced the world. From the scatting of Louis Armstrong, Ella Fitzgerald, and Dizzy Gillespie to the distinctiveness of Lou Rawls and Aretha Franklin to the phrasing of Joe Williams, Billie Holiday, and Nancy Wilson to the rootedness of B.B. King and Bessie Smith. We put the wop in do-wop, introducing three, four, five, and six part harmony. The Motown groups, the Philadelphia sound, and the Memphis, Mississippi, and Chicago blues are internationally acclaimed. Urban rap, which sprang from the folk song and spirituals of Black folks, influences young people across the globe. The political and social content of the best of Black rap is directly connected to the liberating poetry of the 1960s, which proclaimed loud and clear that America was in deep, deep trouble, raging out of control on an anti-Black / anti-people course, and not to be trusted or depended upon.

Many African Americans of my generation receive their intellectual substance, beauty, memories, and bonding traditions from the language of Black writers and poets. The Langston Hughes and Zora Neale Hurston in each of us is unique. They and we took the voices of the church, streets, fields, factories, clubs, offices, homes, projects, playgrounds, locker rooms, restaurants, bedrooms, after-hours joints, hotels, schools and colleges, trains and buses, and placed them in a Colored American, Negro American, Black American, and today's African American context. The Brookses, Walkers,

McKays, Toomers, Haydens, Tolsons, Barakas, Bontemps, Sanchezes, Evanses, Browns, Wrights, Ellisons, Reeds, Walkers, Morrisons, Angelous, Knights, Marshalls, Williams, Kellys, Hineses, Baldwins, Killens, McMillans, Cliftons, Bambaras, Harpers, Lordes, Millers, Jordans, Garveys, DuBoises and countless others of us reached into the souls of Black folks and humanized our pain, joy, suffering, achievements, incompetence, goodness, short and long comings for the world to hear, read, and hopefully understand and grow from. To read, study, and write in the tradition of African American literature is, in itself, enough work for 100 serious Ph.D. programs.

We should not apologize to anyone for the language of Black folks in America. Our language, our voices, are not only legitimate, but right and necessary. Much of our culture is based on language. Any people who are aware of and in control of their own cultural anchors will reproduce and contribute to the language in a developmental manner. Our language is our connector to each other. It is what our mothers, fathers, grandparents, aunts, uncles, cousins, and friends understand and taught us. It is how we share our laughter (Moms Mabley, Redd Fox, and Richard Pryor quickly come to mind). It is with language that we bring in our newborns and bury those who have joined our ancestors.

Languages that work are creative sounds and moving feet, are voices in different colors, are mixed rhythms, and the creating of new words and language structures. Ishmael Reed, Alice Walker, John A. Williams, Toni Morrison, Gwendolyn Brooks, all write in English within a hidden force and beauty. Black folks took the droppings of European language and created a literature, a memory.

Our homegrown churches, with their preaching and music, is where our language lives, grows, and adds vision to our lives. There is a special magic in hearing a preacher and choir vocalize their message in complicated harmonies and rhythms, all proclaiming a better day comin'.

This is not to suggest that as we function in other worlds and words we should not learn other languages; that would be stupid and short-sighted. We have to be able to excel in the languages that oppress us as well as in the languages that we work and create in and that will ultimately be liberating to us. If one is in business, he/she must use the language of commerce; if one is in science, he/she must use scientific language; if one is in sociology, he/she must use the language of populations, cities, and rural communities; if one is in the university, he/she must use academic language. However, the language of one's profession is not a 24-hour tool. The wise of us leave it on the job. If I (as a business person) want to borrow money to create a new business I do not go to a bank, dressed in party clothes or cultural dress and say, "yo, bro I need a loan." No! I prepare a loan package, study the lending record of the bank, make an appointment with a loan officer, wear appropriate business attire, and prepare myself to sell my ideas to the loan officer in "banking" or business language. Generally, the wise of our people do not take the language of commerce home to our less formal settings.

To the degree that a people's liberation is connected to communication, it becomes a self-creating prophecy that one speaks as one is. There are certain words in a language that are debilitating to us, no matter how often they are used. Such a word is *"nigger."* Recently, "nigger" has been amplified and overused in the presentations of many urban rappers and comedians. A nigger, the pitiful and shameful invention of Europeans, cannot be de-stereotyped by using it in another context, even if the users are Black and supposedly politically correct (they are mostly young and unaware). A nigger is a nigger is a nigger is a nigger, and white folks love to hear us denigrate each other. Other words like "bitch," "mutherfucker" and "ho" (whore) also speak loudly to the intellectual and cultural limitations of one's cultural education. One speaks as one is. The purpose of liberation rap is not only to reflect one's reality, it is to transcend it. We can all visualize a "ghetto," but can we conceive of a liberated community? Anybody can rap reality. Only artists have vision of a better world.

English is fast becoming a universal language, but not because of the original uniqueness of its linguistic qualities or the popularity of the way writers use it. English is sweeping the globe due to the power and influence of its originators and primary users. As the "official" language of the United States, it represents the preeminent political, economic, military and commercial (i.e., entertainment) voice (power) presently on this earth. (As a powerful force, the U.S. replaced the former power, England.) That is why oppressed people communicating in English must conquer it and proceed with deliberate speed and accuracy to carve out their own territory of self-expression and visions of a bright tomorrow. Language is a code. Learn to use it, or be used by it.

Toni Morrison, novelist and 1993 recipient of the Nobel Prize in Literature, shared the following insights in her acceptance lecture to the Swedish Academy:

> The systematic looting of language can be recognized by the

tendency of its users to forego its nuanced, complex, mid-
wifery properties for menace and subjugation. Oppressive
language does more than represent violence; it is violence;
does more than represent the limits of knowledge; it limits
knowledge. Whether is obscuring state language is the faux-
language of mindless media; whether it is the proud but
calcified language of the academy or the commodity-driven
language of science; whether it is the malign language of
law-without-ethics, or language designed for the estrange-
ment of minorities, hiding under its racist plunder in its
literary cheek—it must be rejected, altered and exposed. It
is the language that drinks blood, laps vulnerabilities, tucks
its fascist boots under crinolines of respectability and patriotism as it moves relentlessly toward the bottom line and the
bottomed-out mind. Sexist language, racist language, theis-
tic language—all are typical of the policing languages of
mastery, and cannot, do not permit new knowledge or
encourage the mutual exchange of ideas.

For example, there is indeed negative cultural baggage in
the use of the words "master" and "slave." Both words have
entered our vocabulary in a way that is demeaning to people of
African descent. However, if history is honestly and accurately
taught and understood, the word "slave" which is a universal
condition—even today—would not be exclusively attached to
Black folk. This may be changing, but all too often when one
mentions "slave" in any setting one automatically thinks of
African people; conversely, the word "master" gives rise to
visions of white men. This more than anything else denotes the
power of white supremacist thought on English.

We who think about work and play in English have given
this a great deal of thought and strongly suggest that we modify
or change our language when referring to the trading of African
people or any people: (1) rather than use "master," use "traders
in human beings"; and (2) rather than "slave," a more accurate
word would be "enslaved," which speaks of the condition

(hopefully temporary) rather than the person. We all value freedom and liberation, and this distinction may be minor in the voices of those in power. But, as it is believed in the Black community, "what goes around, comes around." To be able to decode a language speaks highly of the user. And one's success in any given society often depends upon one's ability to communicate effectively—in speech and on paper—in the language that has traditionally been used to oppress liberating thoughts.

people Black and stone
be careful of that which is designated beautiful
most of us have been taught from the basements
of other people's minds.
often we mistake stripmining for farming
and that   that truly glows is swept under
the rug of group production.
it is accepted in america that beauty is
thin, long & the color of bubble gum.
few articles generated by the millions are beautiful
except   people.

trust people
one by one
the darker they come
the more you can give your heart,
their experiences most likely are yours
or will be yours.
even within the hue and hueless
among them are those
who have recently lost their ability to recall.

they can hurt you
drop you to your knees with words
much of that which blast from their mouths
is not them   the offense is
they do not know that it is not them
as they rip your heart open
and reduce you to the enemy.

CHILDREN-CENTERED CULTURE

The culture that now guides, influences, and manages the development of too many of our children is highly destructive. This culture's obsession with sex and violence is coming home to roost in the negative and self-destructive actions of millions of young people who live on the edge of a throw-away society. The sexual, psychological, and physical abuse of millions of young people in this country is unprecedented and is eating away at the few remaining moral values.

Who among us was not moved to quiet anger by the utter poverty and wretched living conditions of the nineteen children discovered unsupervised on Chicago's West Side during the winter of 1994?* The high pregnancy rate among teenage girls and drug-addicted women, the crippling homicides that are devastating young Black boys, and the unquenchable hunger for any kind of mind-altering, feel-good drug that takes them away from their urine-soaked realities are no longer front page news in many Black communities.

We walk past the homeless with about as much concern for their welfare as for repairing cracks in sidewalks. Many of our

*The raid on this apartment received national attention in newsmagazines, newspapers, national television news and national talk shows. David Van Biema, "Calcutta, Illinois" *Time* (February 14, 1994).

children populate busy street corners and night spots selling their bodies to maintain a lifestyle that less than twenty years ago would have shocked a nation. Much of this is the result of a greed-driven, materialistic, and commercial culture that is all-consuming and that stresses the ownership of things, people, and ideas that are beyond the reach and comprehension of the unemployed, undereducated, and intellectually impoverished among us. Tie this to the almost systematic economic and social destruction of a good many Black families and we indeed have a crisis on our hands.

We are living in unhealthy times, and our relationships, if they exist at all, are often meaningless social or sexual connections with little substance or commitment beyond frequent wiggles on sheetless beds. Many of our young people have lost the one crucial value-based institution that enabled our people to weather the worst that America threw at us: children-centered extended families. The extended families of Black people in America represented the closest thing we had to the African villages of our foreparents. These Black extended families generally operated out of close-knit Black clubs or churches. Many were mini-schools and learning blocks that nurtured, protected, and guided our young people into healthy, productive, and hope-inspired adults. They were fail-safe zones for the community's children.

We are losing too many of our children to a street culture that eats them like fast food. Our children are at risk in so many ways. Yet all that many parents, politicians, business people, and others have to offer is another study.

When I speak of children-centeredness, I mean a culture-rich community based upon the healthy development of its members from childhood into adulthood—a culture that provides innovative ideas for families and institutions with the ease and frequency that violence and sex are currently highlighted. We need a society that views children as a priority and therefore supports those institutions that support children: families, boys' and girls' clubs, YMCAs and YWCAs, schools, libraries, churches, mosques, temples, etc. As it stands now, the first line in this battle are the confused youngsters who are themselves locked into "get it fast and get it cheap" attitudes. Too many young people look to other young people for answers to problems that their parents are unable or unwilling to deal with. Here are some suggestions:

1. Our youth are having sex too young and under the wrong conditions. Sex education is badly needed and should be provided early to boys and girls in settings that are non-threatening. Young people need to talk about sex with caring, knowledgeable adults before they hit the streets for lessons from "pimps and whores slamming Cadillac doors." Ideally, the parents should provide sex education. However, most parents are incapable or refuse to teach sex education to their own children. Therefore, it must be provided by professionals. Abstinence must be presented as a clear and acceptable option to which much attention is given. In fact, abstinence should be the only option taught at the elementary level. In high school, a combination of abstinence and use of contraceptives should be taught.

2. We must clearly state that it is *not* OK to have children outside of a committed adult relationship, preferably mar-

riage.   Young men and women must be taught   by instruction and example to take responsibility for their sexual lives. However, this is like talking to the wind if young people are not given healthy options. Such options existed thirty years ago in our communities. Not only did more challenging schools exist, but there was life after school in the church, boys and girls clubs, YMCAs and YWCAs, and the many extra curricular activities in which we involved our children, such as sports, music, chess and checker clubs, science clubs, history clubs, and fruitful employment. We must keep our children busy in a creative and healthy way. Television as a baby-sitter is not a viable option, for the values that radiate from the "tube," for the most part, are not life-giving or life-developing. However, if a teenager does have a child, she must be helped because she is a parent with another life in her young hands. The father of the child must be made accountable and made to live up to his responsibilities to the mother and to his child. The families of both teenagers must give loving and understanding support to them and to the baby. A teenager's life does not end because a baby is born out of wedlock. That baby can have a wonderful life with the support of a family. Many times, child and mother grow up together. Those babies that are not aborted need love, attention, and all the elements that create healthy, intelligent, and talented children. None of our children are illegitimate. However, too many are unwanted and unloved.

3.   Crack cocaine and AIDS are the new mega-death carriers that have invaded our communities. Having grown up in a drug-infested home, I know first-hand the pain, hope-

lessness, and fears that children experience daily. This too is why extended family/communities are absolutely necessary. Caring relatives should always be on the watch for the children in their extended families who may live in homes that are at risk. It is imperative that we work for drug-free homes and environments. As I write this essay, the fastest-growing AIDS-infected group is Black women. This again is why sex education and responsible sexual behavior is absolutely necessary. AIDS is not a gay disease and we must confront it as we have other life-threatening infections.

4. Adults who have decided to become family must plan for their children. Children by accident are often raised accidentally, without care or protection. Unwanted children are clearly a major problem facing our communities, and these children face the greatest threat of child abuse and neglect. Potential parents must decide, before conception, the type of life they want for themselves and their children and then put a plan of action into place. Rearing children is one of the most complex and difficult tasks facing us and needs to be uppermost in our minds before we bring them into this very hard and uncaring world. There must be a plan. Such a plan must include informal and formal education provided in secure and caring environments, preferably extended family settings with lots of love and good human examples of a healthy lifestyle. Men must be closely involved in the birth of their children. Often, this is the key element missing in early bonding with one's children. This means that we men need to adopt a life-style that includes our children. Potential factors

include:

a.   Taking child-bearing classes with your wife-mate

b.   Visiting the doctor or midwife with your wife-mate so that he/she understands that you are involved and want to be consulted at all levels of the birth of your child.

c.   During the child's birth, stay with your wife-mate. Hopefully your child will be born in an enlightened hospital or birthing center where you can hold your wife-mate's hand or even get into bed with her. That is, straddling her back as your baby is born so that the two of you will experience this beauty at the same time. In this way you will be able to cut the umbilical cord and hold your baby at the same time as your wife-mate.

5.   The worldwide population problem is quickly affecting the natural resources of this small planet. There are over 6 billion people in the world today and over half of them live in serious poverty. Parents should consciously limit their child-bearing to as few children as possible, most certainly not having more children than they can adequately care for. This is obviously a moral, economic, and political discussion. Clearly, we have too many children who are not being cared for; think about adoption. Become aware of the global population crisis and the role it plays in the destruction of the environment and people. Think about how you as a parent can aid in the reversal and repair of environmental destruction. Remember, good family planning is preventive health for children and parents.

6.   Once children come into our lives, our lives must change

toward centering much of our attention to their healthy development. This requires the creation of a home environment that is safe, clean, fun, challenging, and loving. This requires that when parents "go," they take their children with them whenever possible. Remember, as a parent, you represent the first and most important example for your children. As parents, you are the first-line teacher. All of a parent's time with his/her children is a lesson, even when not meant to be so.

7. Become intimately involved in the extended family/community that practices the values and lifestyle you deem healthy and productive. This extended family-community is both biological and cultural, including close relatives—grandparents, aunts, uncles, and friends, church members, club members, etc. This community arrangement is the closest protective shield that we have to our traditional African villages for rearing children. It is difficult for the whole "village" to raise a child when the "village" does not exist and is peopled with a variety of folks of different values and cultures. Our communities have changed. Yes, the projects and majority Black communities are pretty much the same, but many of us are scattered and are not interested in helping to rear each other's children. We must each create an extended family/community wherever we live. In some cases, this may include people of other ethnic groups.

8. Stay in control. Study parenting. Children need guidance, love and discipline. Such needs will change as they grow, but parents must keep a sensitive ear and heart turned to the

footsteps of their children. Anticipation is the norm.
Always try to think ahead of your children. Study child
development. We are not looking for an all-inclusive road
map for childrearing because all children are different and
require individual needs. But, by studying the literature
and listening to the elders in the community, one acquires
ideas to incorporate into a creative plan. In order for our
children to be mentally and physically healthy, they must
live in an extended family/community that is functioning
beyond the survival mode and well into developmental
activities.

9.   Try to keep your children in growth environments. Whether
they are involved in quality schools, sport activities,
entertainment, travel and/or work, they must always be
busy and challenged. Everything that a child experiences
is the sum total of his or her education and feeds his/her
inner compass. Use and support libraries, summer camps,
computer camps, and any activity that will enable your
child to enjoy his/her childhood while providing him/her
with an introduction to the complexities of this vast world.

10. Being a parent is probably, with the exception of being a
good mate to your partner, the most difficult, complicated
and taxing job in the world if it's done right. There are no
quick fixes to parenting. Too many parents learn "on the
job" and too many have no idea of the complexity involved. Study is in order as well as questioning and
listening to your parents, grandparents and wise elders
from your extended family/community. Always remember, men must be equal parents. Conscious fatherhood

should become a given fact in families where children exist.

11. Parents, as mentioned above, will be the primary influence upon and examples for children. Develop healthy lifestyles. It is difficult to lie to children. That which is negative about your life will come out. Contradictions are like open wounds covered by band-aids. Work on your shortcomings. For example, it is almost a fruitless activity to constantly preach the harmful effects of smoking, violence, irresponsible sexual conduct, or drug use to your children if your life is consumed by such debilitating actions and habits. Child abuse, whether it is sexual, physical or emotional, remains a major problem in this country. Parents need help and children need protection. This is where billions of dollars need to go for prevention in the form of pre-schools, parenting classes, support groups for abusive parents and children.

12. Children need nonviolent homes, communities, learning structures, play environments, and places of worship. Solutions to problems must be achieved in a nonviolent manner. Mothers and fathers must not solve their problems with fistfights or verbal abuse. Children must observe and be a part of nonviolent conflict resolutions. Violence has entered our homes in many ways, but television remains the chief transmitter. Its use must be carefully monitored. Remember, mass media is not a responsible media. Those individuals who work in mass media do not always look out for the best interests of children. Also, with the coming of the electronic highway, we need

to prepare for the unexpected. At a minimum, this preparation must include more careful monitoring of children's interactions with not only television, but with other instruments of high technology.

13. As our children grow, we must accommodate their needs. Our homes must be mini-learning institutions. Books, music, culturally reflective art work, positive, value-based videos and magazines must be a part of our homes. We have to creatively shower our children in a developmental Black culture. It is critical that cultural knowledge is communicated and taught early. Quality is the key concept in all that we do: quality in our decision making, quality in the implementation, quality in the work, quality in our love, quality in our vision and quality in our decisions and expectations.

14. We need baby sitting cooperatives in communities where mothers have to work. Parents need to support parents. Parents must be involved in their children's activities—especially in their schools. If our children are to do well in school, parents must be involved. Visit your child's school or day-care center. We must show supreme interest in everything that our children do. If education is truly a tool for liberation and economic mobility, we parents must also be lifelong students. The best example for our children is their observation of our self-improvement.

15. Before parents bring children into the world, they must understand family and parenting. Parents must be the number-one advocates for our children; however, if they

have no concept of what their roles involve, then we are in deep trouble. Family should represent the most secure, loving, and dependable institutions that our children know.

16. A National Child Day, or for certain within our communities a National Black Child Day, should be established. A day to celebrate children. This would bring together churches, service organizations, educators, business women and men to discuss children/care and development *only* and to come up with concrete plans to reduce the stress upon and "oppression" of children. Parents and professionals should form committees for session follow-ups. This should be a non-commercial day. A national Black child day could be co-sponsored by Black churches, sororities and fraternities, and child advocacy groups.

17. Develop an oppression-free home/community. The number one health problem in the Black community is stress. Children experience stress also. Are we adults putting too much pressure on our children? Are our expectations unrealistic? Do our children have enough support? Are we disciplining our children in a healthy way? Are we teaching nonviolent conflict resolution? Are we solving problems with conversation and communication? However, this does not mean that we lower our expectations of our children. Always challenge them in a healthy way.

18. Develop "culture-proud" homes in which our children are deeply oriented into their own culture in a nondegrading manner. This requires that the parents are comfortable as Black people, knowledgeable about their African heritage and aware of their connection to and role in America.

19. Our children should be taught to be proud of themselves early. They should be made to understand that they are normal and that the differences that exist between people and are not necessarily bad. They need to be able to understand the "positiveness" of their color and their African heritage. Derogatory terms used to refer to Black people should not be used. Self-esteem in children is a growth process; parents must have it too. In a white supremacist culture, Black parents will have to work at providing a positive cultural home and education for their children. There is no substitute for twenty-four hour love and an environment rich with positive cultural reinforcement for children, e.g., people, art, books, music, etc.

20. We need to listen to young people. Media needs to provide air time and print space to air young people's concerns and points of view. There needs to be citywide converstions between young people.

21. As a writer and father, I intimately understand the power of the arts. Our children should be introduced to the arts: music, dance, visual art, literature, and the positive affects of popular culture (e.g. not all rap is negative). Encourage young people to be creative, to develop their artistic talents.

22. Learn from your errors. Let your mistakes be a lesson. However, be honest with your children if you are not sure of something. Be quick to apologize when you have wronged them. Teach them to understand that to error is to be human. No one is mistake free. However, although perfection does not exist, we must always work to become

the best. Our goal is to be "world class" in almost everything we do.

It is urgent that we become child-centered as individuals, families, communities, nation, and world. If you do not want to give quality attention to the development of your children, do not have any children. We do not have a choice. Our children are living in very dangerous times and they need much more than the bare necessities for them to mature into healthy and productive adults. If they do not get this nurturing, it is almost certain that we will end up repairing broken adults, visiting our children in hospitals and prisons, or digging early graves for them. Few acts are as painful or debilitating as burying a daughter or son. This is our call—will we answer?

Suggested Readings:

Billingsley, Andrew. *Climbing Jacob's Ladder: The Enduring Legacy of African American Families* (New York: Simon and Schuster), *1993*.

Dosh, Leon. *When Children Want Children* (New York: Morrow), 1989.

Hare, Nathan and Julia. *The Endangered Black Family* (San Francisco: The Black Think Tank), *1984*.

Warfield-Coppock, Nsenga. *Adolescent Rites of Passage* (Washington, D.C.: Baobab Associates, Inc.), *1990*.

Wade Nobles and his associates at the Institute for the Advanced Study of Black Family Life and Culture have produced a wealth of material on the family that I highly recommend. They can be reached at P.O. Box 24739 Oakland, California 94623.

BLACKS, JEWS AND
HENRY LOUIS GATES, JR.

S eldom has a Black intellectual been as recruited, pampered, patronized, positioned, empowered, lied to, and anointed as Henry Louis Gates, Jr. Professor Gates, known as "Skip" to his friends, previously of Duke, Cornell, Yale, and Oxford, is now simultaneously chairman of Harvard's African-American Studies department, director of the W. E. B. Du Bois Institute, and the W. E. B. Du Bois Professor of Humanities. He is also the major voice for the anti-Black, pro-white/Jewish wing of the academic and political middle—located primarily on the east coast of the country.

Never in the history of Black-white relationships in the United States has an African American been given such unrestricted, unlimited access to influential white journals, newspapers, magazines, and quarterlies. His articles and reviews are not just filler material, equal to that of other scholars or writers, but are often the cover pieces—giving Mr. Gates a tremendous amount of influence and power in the arena of ideas. However, this privilege is within context. The area in which Gates has emerged as the "unchallenged" authority is Black Studies (i.e. Black folks). It doesn't matter what the subject, or where the Black folks reside, or under what conditions, if white media needs a comment, Mr. Gates is now in front of the line—far ahead of Shelby Steele, Stephen L. Carter, Cornel West, Manning Marable, Thomas Sowell, and Glenn Loury.

In the span of six weeks, I have read three of his articles/ reviews in major publications: the *New York Times Book Review* - front page (12 September 1993), cover article for the *New Republic* (20 September 1993), and commentary in the *Economist* (11 September 1993). What emerges here is an uncensored voice, supposedly with a critical and unique "Black" position that will give whites and others a critical "insider's" view of the Black world. His voice is all over the place (more about this later). What has been created here is a modern day, 21st-century, updated Booker T. Washington. Mr. Washington was used and reused by whites to promote their line of thought and to act as buffer between Black folks and the radical ideas of W. E. B. Du Bois and others. At least Mr. Washington left us Tuskegee University. What will Mr. Gates leave us?

Dr. Gates is undoubtedly a gifted and learned scholar. In 1973 he graduated *suma cum laude* from Yale. He was one of the first African Americans to earn a Ph.D. at Cambridge University and was a tenured professor at Cornell before the age of 34. He is best known for his book *The Signifying Monkey*, which won him the American Book Award in 1989. His other books are *Figures in Black: Words, Signs, and the "Racial" Self* and *Loose Cannons: Notes on the Culture Wars*. His edited and co-edited works are in the double digits. With the recently published Amistad Literary series, co-edited with his protege K. Anthony Appiah, Gates, without question, dominates the field of Black literary criticism. The award that freed him financially and secured his "genius" status was a MacArthur Foundation fellowship. The MacArthur Foundation gave him the intellectual freedom to take chances and become truly "independent" in the Western intellectual context, enabling him to textually follow the imagination of others.

His intellectual output has been remarkable; one wonders if he sleeps. In 1993, he published over 18 articles, book reviews, and commentary. His works have been published in such diverse publications as *Time, Newsday, The New Yorker, Forbes,* the *Washington Post,* the *Nation,* the *New Republic, Sports Illustrated,* and, of course, the *New York Times,* where he seems to be in residency. He is interviewed on some aspect of the Black situation weekly, and if there is a major event such as Toni Morrison winning the Nobel Prize in literature, you can be sure the *New York Times* will have his remarks. In fact, it was a *New York Times Magazine* cover story (7 April 1990) that gave him his wings. As he glared intently on the cover, one could almost hear him say, "Watch me now!"

However, what is even more remarkable is that a scholar with such a high profile and extensive publication record has so few detractors or critics in print. There are tons of dissatisfaction and criticism that have been voiced about Mr. Gates by colleagues, students, employees, and writers off the record. Selase Williams, former chair of the National Council for Black Studies, and Molefi Asante, chair of the African Studies department at Temple University, are among the few who are quoted in print.

Some criticism from Black feminists was beginning to hit the fan a few years ago, but much of that was squelched with his editing of *Reading Black, Reading Feminist* (1990). Some of his critics were included in the volume, and those who were left out were effectively neutralized. The only thorn in his brain and white heart has come from the Black woman literary critic, Joyce A. Joyce. Dr. Joyce has had the impudence to question the integrity, quality, and originality of the works of Dr. Gates and Houston Baker. (You can read this exchange in *New Literary History*, Vol. 18, No. 2, Winter 1987.)

Mr. Gates has presence, and his bite, I'm told, does strike fear into the hearts and minds of many "wannabe" scholars (obviously, there is a big contradiction here), assistant professors fighting for tenure, young writers looking for publishing contracts and grants, and first book authors looking for a jacket blurb to help sales. It is clear that Dr. Gates is frequently called upon to pass judgment on the "new Negroes," and his stamp of approval may be the difference between a fast or slow future. His signature on one's recommendation carries considerable weight among those that matter in the white world.

In his 1987 essay, *"What's Love Got To Do With It?: Critical Theory, Integrity, and the Black Idiom,"* Dr. Gates states in his answer to Dr. Joyce's criticism:

> Let me state clearly that I have no fantasy about my readership: I write for our writers and for our critics... But no, I do not think that my task as a critic is to lead black people to "freedom." My task is to explicate Black texts. That's why I became a critic.

If this was really the case, the problem Dr. Gates poses for the Black community would be minimal. Gates cannot be dismissed as a "rank opportunist or intellectual mercenary." He is in keeping with the Western scholarly tradition where they eat each other for lunch and play the dozens with a smile haboring razor blades between their teeth. His intellectual talents and critical skills are real enough. It is his values, perspective and willingness to go outside of his discipline at the expense of Black folks that makes him dangerous and suspect.

In his *New York Times* op-ed article (20 July 1992), "Black Demagogues and Pseudo-Scholars," Gates has forsaken literary criticism for anti-Black political commentary suggesting to readers that he is (1) a specialist on Black-Jewish relationships, and (2) a historian. I am unaware of his scholarly credentials in either field. Dr. Gates' essay, unknown to most, is more of a companion piece to the ADL Research Report,* "The Anti-Semitism of Black Demagogues and Extremists," issued in early 1992. Gates' ideological thrust is the same as the ADL report. His essay is critically important for many reasons, not only for what it addresses but for what it leaves out. The intent of the essay is to state and question the growth of anti-Semitism, as well as Black demagogues and pseudo-scholars, in the Black community.

With this in mind, consider these points:

1. The *New York Times* is, without question, the most influential paper in the country. The *New York Times* is a

---

* ADL is not a politically pure organization. In fact, according to the latest information to emerge, the ADL has been spying on both its enemies and its friends. According to Abdeen Jabara, "for decades the Anti-Defamation League B'nai B'rith has run a private nationwide spy network—a systematic, long-term, professionally organized political espionage operation complete with informers, infiltrators, money laundering, code names, wire tapping and secret meetings. While it is not unusual for private political groups to gather information, the ADL spying is different. It is not only the scale which sets it apart—files on 950 organizations and nearly 10,000 individuals—but the focus. The ADL spied on groups which opposed its stated goals as well as those which supported its principles. More disturbing, however, is the League's collaboration with state, federal and foreign intelligence gathering entities. This sharing of often confidential information and resources is not only illegal, but a violation of trust, a threat to civil liberties and an infringement on the right to privacy." ("The Anti-Defamation League: Civil Rights and Wrongs," *Covert Action*, Summer 1993, No. 45.)

family-owned paper and the family is Jewish. The current publisher is Arthur Ochs Sulzberger, Jr., who succeeded his father as publisher about two years ago. The *New York Times*' record of objectivity and impartiality is supposed to be beyond question. However, like most media in the U.S., the *New York Times* has its own political and social agenda. Most Blacks (and others) do not necessarily buy into its motto, "All the News that's fit to Print."

2.   For the *New York Times* to devote an entire page of its op-ed section to a Black scholar is unprecedented. In fact, few white commentators could demand such space. If Mr. Gates had written on any aspect of positive Black development, at most he may have received a column. For him to narrowly focus on what he perceives as a national problem, "Black Anti-Semitism," is either naive or opportunistic. Such an assertion is simply not true; there is no reliable research that can document this so-called re-emergence of Black anti-Semitism among African Americans, nor can anyone document any time in our history in which Black anti-Semitism was a problem. That some Blacks are anti-Jewish cannot be denied, but to state that it is a national problem is as ridiculous as believing in the tooth fairy. I do not know of any Blacks who have disputed the existence of the Jewish Holocaust or the significance of the Jewish struggle for empowerment within the white tribal structure. So much for scholarship.

3.   The neoconservative movement in this country over the last twelve years, using such diverse publications as the *Spotlight*, *Commentary*, *New Republic*, the *New York*

Times, and others, continues to use Blacks to push a reactive position of Black victimization—as if most Blacks spend their time thinking about whites or Jews, cheating the government, or trying not to work, rather than trying to move themselves and their families toward some level of self-reliance, economic stability, and peace. (See Andrew Billingsley's *Climbing Jacob's Ladder.*) With over 800,000 Black men locked up in the nation's prisons, it seems to me that white supremacy (racism) is a major problem that needs to be addressed in full page essays in the *New York Times* and elsewhere.

4. Why is it when white folks or Jews (who are white too) have a problem with Blacks, they pull out of their bags any number of Negroes to "read us the riot act?" Mr. Gates' essay did not just come about because of his concern for Black anti-Semitism. Rather, it is a well-thought-out tactical maneuver to ingratiate himself with the powerful side of the Jewish community at the expense of Black folks. It's something like Bill Clinton calling out Sister Souljah to embarrass Jesse Jackson and garner the white vote. Therefore, Gates' strategy to go after Minister Farrakhan, John Henrik Clarke and others of less influence, as if they were chosen or elected spokesmen for the 35 million African American citizens in this country, is without logic. I have never read in the pages of any respected publication any single voice from the Irish, Polish, Anglo-Saxon, or Jewish communities being allowed to misrepresent their people based on the alleged comments of a few.

5. Mr. Gates speaks and writes as if no Jews are racist. Has
    he not been reading and studying the works and statements
    of Norman Podhoretz, Richard Herrnstein, Joseph Epstein,
    Martin Peretz and others? These neoconservative Jews and
    others have led the attack against any kind of Black devel-
    opment over the last fifteen years or so. This is not to deny
    the important work of Jewish progressives in the country.

6. Whose interest is really served by this so-called rise in
    Black anti-Semitism? Is such a charge intended to put
    Black folks in bed with the white right? Is much of this
    name calling a reaction to what is happening in New York
    City—where Jews reside in large numbers and in close
    proximity to Black folks—and an attempt, by faulty
    reasoning, to transform that volatile situation into a
    national problem? It is obvious to thinking people that the
    real threat to Jews is the same one they have been experi-
    encing throughout their history: the Aryan nation, Nazi
    Skinheads, the Klu Klux Klan, Christian fundamentalists,
    and the rise of extremist white supremacist culture among
    many poor white youth. I suggest that Mr. Gates read
    Blood in the Face by James Ridgeway and one of the
    "bibles" of the white right, *The Turner Diaries* by Andrew
    MacDonald. If he is serious about knowing who the real
    racists and anti-Semites are, I also recommend *The Silent
    Brotherhood* by Kevin Flynn and Gary Gerhardt, *Brother-
    hood of Murder* by Thomas Martinez and John Guinther,
    and *Bitter Harvest* by James Corcoran.

7. What was missing from Mr. Gates' analysis was a possi-
    bility of a Jewish-Islamic confrontation being played out

in the United States. Minister Farrakhan— who has ties to Libya's Colonel Quaddafi—is also a Muslim. Most certainly for the last fifty years, the State of Israel and most of the Arab-Islamic world has been in a state of "war." Could not the new difficulty many Jews experience as a result of Minister Farrakhan's remarks and existence be viewed as part the classic religious battle between Judaism and Islam, between Jews and Muslims. By elevating Minister Farrakhan to the level of "leader" of Black people, Gates —by extension—endows Mr. Farrakhan as leader of all of us (which is not true). But, in the final countdown, Minister Farrakhan cannot remotely approach the power or influence posed by Jerry Falwell, David Duke, Pat Robertson, Pat Buchanan, or any number of Christian right representatives in America.

8. In the Winter 1993/1994 issue of *Black Books Bulletin,* we published the response of the respected and honored historian John Henrik Clarke. The *New York Times* would not consider publishing his response to Mr. Gates. So much for "fair" journalism. Professor Clarke has lived over half a century in New York City and closely worked with Jews during much of this time. His insights on New York Jews cannot be easily dismissed because the literary influence of Jews is phenomenal. For another view of this read Richard Kostelanetz's *Literary Politics in America,* especially the first half of the book. Has the *New York Times* ever devoted an entire op-ed page to white racism or white anti-Semitism written by whites or Blacks? No, absolutely not. Only Black folks screaming to the white choir will be permitted such space to analyze and comment

on so-called Black anti-Semitism, Black anti-Asianism, Black anti-Latinoism and Black anti-Blackism. The victim analyzing the victim for the perpetrator. I suggest that Mr. Gates, if he is indeed a scholar, study the publications of John Henrik Clarke, whose essays have been published widely (most recently his books *Christopher Columbus and the African Holocaust, African People and World History* and *Notes for an African World Revolution*).

9. Just as some Blacks use racism as a shield against all criticism from non-Blacks, whether it is legitimate or not, many Jews have hidden behind anti-Semitism to escape any real criticism of their own racism and failings. I matured during the Black Struggle of the 1960s and I know first-hand the contribution many Jews made to our movement, but does that mean that they can do no wrong? It seems as though the only criticism Jews will accept or consider is that from other Jews. Most Jews have long and unforgiving memories. For example, Jesse Jackson misspoke and acquired the wrath of many Jews. This was about six years ago, and he still has not been forgiven. Jesse Jackson could genuflect on his thumbs, perform a thousand salahs to the earth, travel to Israel and kneel at the Wailing Wall for forgiveness and still a significant number of powerful Jews would never forgive him for his remarks. However, on the other hand, Pat Buchanan, who has gone a thousand yards past Jesse Jackson in his criticism of Jews does not have to endure organized criticism. Is there a double standard? Yes, there is not a master-slave relationship with Pat Buchanan as with Jesse Jackson, and Jackson is being persecuted for going beyond his assigned role as "negro leader."

10. Part of this battle is actually between multi-culturalism and African-centered studies. Most Blacks agree that African-centered studies is about the intellectual empowerment of Blacks. One cannot talk about multiculturalism or the benefits of sharing cultures if all one has to bring to the table is the back-lot buckdancing from Europe that occupies most Black minds. Most of the formal education Blacks receive (90%) is based upon a Western educational model. All Blacks worldwide have experienced serious brain mismanagement. Just as Jews have recaptured their minds and have little difficulty defining and supporting Jewish life or Jewish studies, thinking Blacks feel the same way. African Americans all over the country, in and out of academia, are seeking new thought and new paradigms using Africa as a starting point rather than Europe. This is not a recent struggle; it started over a century ago. During the 1960s, the literary side of this struggle was led by poets, writers and critics. Hoyt W. Fuller, Darwin T. Turner, and Addison Gayle, Jr. gave their lives to this movement. We must keep the tradition alive.

As a poet-activist-educator-businessman for about 30 years, I have been able to be a part of and feel the heartbeat of my people. In the talking drum from Black barber and beauty shops to Sunday morning church services, seldom, if ever, is there any significant discussion about Jews. When we do talk about white folks, Jews are on an equal footing with Italians, Irish, Polish, and other whites. Yes, cultural and religious distinctions sometime come into the discussion such as the Irish Catholics retaking of city hall in Chicago after the unexpected death of Mayor Harold Washington.

If one is honest (and this is at a premium these days) and seriously explores the literature on Black-Jewish relations over the last fifty years, one will notice that it is literature written primarily by Jews. There has been only one single-author book published on Black-Jewish relationships prior to *The Secret Relationship Between Blacks and Jews,* which was produced by committee. Black writers have contributed to edited works and some have included a chapter or passages in their works, but James Samuel Stemons' *As Victim to Victims: An American Negro Laments with Jews* (1941) is the first and only book by a Black author that I am aware of. On the other hand, I have in my library over 22 books written or edited by Jewish authors that examine the "Negro/Black-Jewish question." The number of Jewish writers producing books exclusively on the "Black question" falls into the hundreds. The intellectual problem is that the criticism has been one-sided and Mr. Gates jumps to the side of the critics. Supposedly, Dr. Gates is displaying "objectivity," Negro liberalism, and scholarship as he earns his brownie points.

Dr. Gates' essay, in all of its distortions, has become the reference article of record in most debates about Black anti-Semitism, compounding distortion upon distortion. He and Cornel West (who is writing a book on Blacks and Jews with the *TIKKUN* editor Michael Lerner) continue to promote distortions of Black-Jewish relationships in the pages of *Emerge* magazine and their articles were published together on the op-ed pages of the *New York Times* (14 April 1993). There are approximately 6 million Jews in America and 35 million Blacks and more Blacks work for Jews than Jews work for Blacks. Who has the problem? Who is the producer and who is the consumer? Why are we not talking about the Black-Irish problem, the Black-Polish problem, or the Black-Italian problem? I strongly suggest that Drs. Gates and West spend more time in the community they say they represent.

Dr. Gates now travels the Jewish Temple an white college circuit giving speeches on the "problem." Third World Press, the publishing company I founded has entered Dr. Gates' stump speeches in a rather negative way due to our publishing of Michael Bradley's *Chosen People From The Caucasus: Jewish Origins, Delusions, Deceptions, and Historical Role in the Slave Trade, Genocide and Cultural Colonization.* Third World Press is 26 years old and believes in the First Amendment (which Gates wrote a cover story on for the *New Republic*) and will continue to publish controversial works as long as they are factual, well-reasoned, tightly-argued, and contribute to African world development. Third World Press has published hundreds of books by authors from the United States to Africa. The one time that we published a white author is the only time a mention of our works has graced the precious lips of Mr. Gates. This is somewhat odd for a man who is projected as the pre-eminent Black literary critic, since the great majority of Third World Press publications fall in the category of creative literature.

I'll never forget the contribution to our culture and struggle made by Hoyt W. Fuller. Mr. Fuller was the managing editor of the monthly journal *Negro Digest*, renamed *Black World* in the 1970s. *Black World* was the most important journal of Black ideas published since the *Crisis* under the editorship of W. E. B. Du Bois. The writers and thinkers among our people from Alice Walker, Ishmael Reed, Toni Cade Bambara, Sonia Sanchez, Wole Soyinka, Toni Morrison, John A. Williams,

Gwendolyn Brooks, Harold Cruse, Margaret Walker, James Baldwin, John O. Killens, to hundreds of others filled its pages. However, Mr. Fuller was fired because of his politics and *Black World*, a Johnson publication was discontinued by Mr. Johnson (who also is the publisher of *Ebony*, *Jet* and *EM*).

I was in the leadership of a group that organized a nation-wide boycott of Johnson publications to protest this action. John Henrik Clarke and many others, converged on Chicago to participate in this demonstration. We set up picket lines in front of the new Johnson headquarters. Mr. Johnson had just opened a multi-storied office building downtown on Michigan Avenue. A first for Blacks in Chicago. We were not an hour into our demonstration when John Johnson, himself, came outside and asked that we come upstairs to talk about his decision. We stopped our mass actions and went into the boardroom at Johnson Publishing Company. Two questions were put on the table: (1) why was Hoyt Fuller fired? (2) and why had *Black World* ceased publishing? Johnson's answer was shocking. He stated that Fuller was fired because he refused to cease publishing the Palestinian side of the Middle-East struggle and the African support of that struggle. He ceased the publication of *Black World* mainly because Jewish businessmen threatened to pull their advertising out of *Ebony* and *Jet* magazines and would have convinced their white friends to do the same if the Middle East coverage did not stop. We were stunned into a weakening silence. Our responses were few because we knew it was both an economic and political decision and that as an astute businessman, Johnson had done what he felt was best for his company. We left and many of us formed a group to start *First World* magazine under the editorship of Hoyt Fuller.

This Jewish-Black relationship was a wake-up call to Black activists about the economic and political power of the Jewish community. However, for John Henrik Clarke, our elder, it was not a new revelation and he began to teach and write about that side of history on a more frequent basis. When SNCC took up the issue of the Palestinian Struggle, it also lost Jewish support and had to close its doors due to this and other problems. Jews, like all people who are in control of their own cultural imperatives, act in self-protective ways, 24-hours a day, each day of the year, without apology. This is as it should be. To minimize the political, economic, cultural power, and influence of Jews is to display an appalling ignorance. (See my essay "Black and Jews: The Continuing Question" in *Black Men: Obsolete, Single, Dangerous?*)

This issue of anti-Semitism is a difficult one and has a long well-documented history. Jewish development in America also has been, and continues to be, a struggle. Black anti-Semitism has not been an impediment or a serious issue in the Jewish rise to prominence and power in the United States. I strongly suggest that Mr. Gates, the scholar that he is, study the literature. Here are a few books he should start with: *The New Conservatives* edited by Lewis A. Coser and Irving Howe, *Anti-Semitism: A Disease of the Mind* by Theodore Issac Rubin, *Where are We: The Inner Life of America's Jews* by Leonard Fein, *The Non-Jewish Jew and Other Essays* by Issac Deutscher, *New York's Jewish Jew: The Orthodox Community in the Interwar Years* by Jenna Weissman Joselit, *The Jewish Writer in America: Assimilation and the Crisis of Identity* by Allen Guttman, *An Empire of their Own: How the Jews Invented Hollywood* by Neal Gabler, *Israel in America: A Too-*

Comfortable Exile? by Jacob Neusner, *Jewish Publishing in America: The Impact of Jewish Writing on American Culture* by Charles A. Madison, *The Thirteenth Tribe* by Arthur Koestler, *Lopez of Newport: Colonial American Merchant Prince* by Stanley F. Chyet, and *The Jewish Presence: Essays on Identity and History* by Lucy Dawidowicz.

It is interesting and no less mysterious to ask why we do not see prominent white scholars writing about Irish anti-Semitism, German, Italian, and/or Polish anti-Semitism on the Op-ed pages of the *New York Times* with the same type of coverage as so-called Black anti-Semitism. After all, the Europeans were the ones who almost wiped the Jews from the face of the earth.

As far as Gates is concerned, much of this comes together for me when in the spring of 1993, Henry Louis Gates, Jr. was awarded the George Polk award. This award is given yearly to the journalist who contributes significantly to the fight against anti-Semitism. In his acceptance remarks, Gates stated:

> I am so very moved and honored to be recognized in the company of so many great journalists; I guess I feel like a bit of cubic zirconia in a diamond mine. So, let me thank the genuine article: my editor of the *New York Times* Op-Ed pages, Howard Goldberg and, of course, Mitchel Levitas.

As a journalist, Gates failed. However, such failure does bring recognition, new allies, awards, prestige, payment, distinction, publishing opportunities, grants, patrons, and the satisfaction that he is, as the *New York Times* proclaims: "Henry Louis Gates, Jr. Black Studies New Star." Welcome to prime time, Skip. At what cost?

THE FARRAKHAN FACTOR

The Question That Will Not Go Away

A round mid-April 1983, on a Saturday afternoon, the city of Baltimore was preparing to receive a visit from the new leader of the Nation of Islam (NOI), Minister Louis Farrakhan. The week prior to his visit, local radio stations had been announcing the minister's "talk to the community." A coalition of Baltimore organizations, which included Black Nationalists, Black Muslims, youth workers and others co-sponsored the event. Brother Kwame Achebe and other brothers of the Baltimore Black Nationalist/activist community waited patiently as the NOI Fruit of Islam searched each person before admittance to Walbrook High School. Once inside, Brother Kwame, Brother Okigbo, and hundreds of others settled down for what was to be a three hour lecture-sermon on the condition of Black men and women in America.

Every three to four feet inside the auditorium a member of the NOI's Fruit of Islam stood at military attention. These young Black men in dark suits and bow ties (the official uniform of the NOI) were a mixture of locals and out-of-towners. The "new" Nation was still in a rebuilding process, and it was not unusual for brothers in the surrounding areas to work security when the minister was appearing anywhere in the vicinity. However, many of the Baltimore men—young, proud, and serious—were from the same neighborhood that cultured and nurtured Brother Kwame. They were there to protect, serve, praise, listen, learn, and even die for their leader, Minister Louis Farrakhan. Brothers Kwame and Okigbo and others were there to listen and ask questions.

After two and a half to three hours of intense political-religious preaching (some called it theater), the floor was opened for questions. Brother Kwame stood quickly with hand in the air and was immediately recognized. He had listened carefully and intensely to Farrakhan's words. Although he had been formulating his question for about an hour, the core of his concerns had been with him for eighteen years. "Minister Farrakhan," he asked, "taking into account the movement of Black people in America, looking at our history from enslavement, post-enslavement, through the Garvey movement up to the 1960s, at any given time, individuals have made a great difference in our development. I mentioned Marcus Garvey, there too were W.E.B. Du Bois, Booker T. Washington, Paul Robeson, Elijah Muhammad, Malcolm X, and countless others. I'm wondering why it was necessary in your lecture to denigrate the life, meaning, and memory of Minister Malcolm X, even as you call for unity?" Minister Farrakhan's answer was slow but deliberate, "Brother Kwame, we felt it necessary to protect our father's name. In the eyes of many, Malcolm X had replaced the Honorable Elijah Muhammad as the primary force in the NOI and I needed to tell our side of history."

Brother Kwame, still on his feet and clearly not satisfied with the answer, immediately pushed for a follow-up: "Minister Farrakhan, in terms of the assassination of Minister Malcolm, would you please explain to us your connection, if any, and..." Before Brother Kwame could finish his sentence the FOI moved swiftly toward him. As they moved, so did Brother Okigbo and others to cover Kwame's back. Tens of other brothers jumped to their feet to stand with Kwame as Brother Okigbo hollered out, "There is not going to be any stuff in here tonight!" Minister Farrakhan, seeing a possible situation that could prove embarrassing, stepped in. "My Brother Kwame," he responded, "you have asked one of the most important and profound questions facing Black America. What is the truth about the killing of Minister Malcolm X? Such a question requires a forum unto itself and I promise that when I return to Baltimore that is a question I will address."

At that point, the stage was cleared and Kwame's question floated in the air bouncing between the conversations of men and women as they exited Walbrook High School. There was no follow-up forum held on that key question in Baltimore or any other city.

Framing the Questions

Seldom does a day pass that the NOI is not in the news. The recent *TIME* cover story (February 28, 1994) is only the latest barrage against Minister Farrakhan and the NOI. The three-part series in the *New York Times* (March 1994) and the cover story in the *Village Voice* (February 15, 1994) have done little to bring understanding to the current debate.

In the hardcore Black community, Minister Farrakhan is not the enemy. Many Black community residents—from Englewood, California, Southside Chicago, Harlem, New York, Westside Detroit, to anywhere U.S.A. where Black folks are undergoing racial, political, and economic destruction—view him as a significant voice. Many also consider him their leader.

The fix on Farrakhan is that he is under attack. I can state without much doubt that the great majority of Black folks did not read the negative pronouncements on Farrakhan and the NOI that appeared in *TIME*, the *New York Times,* or the *Village Voice*. Traditionally, when Black folks are under attack by white folks—especially when it is seeping down from the most powerful media conglomerate on earth—we hang together.

The NOI is not going away, nor should it. There are many problems within and with the NOI, but the need for it far outweighs the problems. Its existence, historical and contemporary, is a fact, and if life is a growth process, the NOI will weather this storm. Anytime a man, such as Farrakhan, can go into a non-home-based city and attract ten thousand or more people, he is speaking a truth to them. And this truth will be defined by the speaker as well as the listeners without outside interpretations. To think that such popularity is only cosmetic, because the majority of the listeners will not join the NOI, is to miss the point: Farrakhan is bringing a message that many, if not most, Black folks can identify with. Why? Because most of us are not crazy. We take from the message that which is valuable, beneficial, developmental, and transcending, and leave the rest at the podium. This is what all intelligent people do who have to function daily at crisis level. Does anyone really believe that if America was *right* that Farrakhan and the NOI would be able to live and grow at such a phenomenal pace?

Some basic understandings:

1. Young Black people are attracted to Minister Farrakhan and the NOI for the same reasons I and many of my generation were attracted to Malcolm X and the NOI. He has touched a sensitive but foundational core of truth in the

young, as they understand it: racism and powerlessness. No other Black leader speaks to the "white man" the way Farrakhan does, in a language that is just on the other side of rap. Malcolm taught him well; the right language is power if used wisely.

2. Most Black folk will not join the NOI. But, just as we supported the NOI when Malcolm was its spokesman, the same is happening with Minister Louis Farrakhan. Most Black folks realize that a radical, militant, uncompromising voice and example is needed to balance the leagues of Negroes and Negro organizations that benefit from our suffering. This is not by any means to suggest that all is right with the NOI . As it was thirty years ago, thinking Black people have serious criticism of the NOI. (More about this later.)

3. Like Malcolm X, Farrakhan was not given to us by white folks. He has not received the USA stamp of approval. His credentials are not from the "best" white universities. His documentation is in the hearts and minds of the Black community and not Europe. His message is conveyed in a truly Black style. It is theater, it is comic relief, it is biblical metaphor raised to the high art of the evangelist. In his message can be found fundamental truths and consistencies. He has taken the Black church on the road, depending as much on the *Bible* as on the *Koran*.

4. Like Malcolm X, Jesse Jackson and Ben Chavis, Farrakhan's ultimate taskmaster is God or Allah. Due to the political nature of our existence in the U.S., it is often forgotten—rather conveniently—that he is a spiritual

leader. If he was just talking politics and economics in the Black community, he would not survive because most Black folks do not trust politicians and bankers. Jesse Jackson's staying power is the Black church. Whether Jackson or Farrakhan is right or wrong, there is always redemption in the Black Church. Farrakhan may be a teacher of the *Koran*, but you can be sure the *Bible* is not far away.

5.   Farrakhan speaks for those who cannot speak for themselves. Here, I am not talking just about the silent oppressed masses, but about the brothers and sisters locked into corporate America, filing documents in federal jobs, walking guard on the borders of Korea, teaching in America's universities, pushing papers and cleaning toilets in local, state, and government jobs and patrolling the streets in the uniforms of law enforcement agencies all over the country.

Therefore, when Kwame Achebe or I ask Minister Farrakhan a question, it is not an attack (question). It is not a question to embarrass or intended to be used by the enemies of Black folks to split us even more. We all start from the same premise—we love our people and only want the best for them. We would be less than critical and intelligent to think that Minister Farrakhan knows what is on the minds of the Kwames of the world. When they do speak up, they do it in a forum filled with Black folks. That gesture represents the highest level of respect. The problem now is that the questions have escaped the confines of the church, temple, mosque, community centers, meeting places, Black bookstores and street corners and

entered into the national media. If it is left to *TIME* and
York Times to frame the questions—you can be absolutely
certain that they will answer them also. This is Farrakhan's
dilemma, and it is ours too. ✗✗✗

Some Little Told History

I do not come to this issue as a nonparticipatory observer.
Most people who know me and/or my work understand the
significant influence that Malcolm X has had on my life. I've
dedicated many of my books and published poems and essays
in respect to his life. I've said many times in public and in
private that of the men who emerged in the 1960s, I credit
Malcolm X with liberating my voice and planting the seed of
commitment to building independent Black institutions in me.
Malcolm X's foresight regarding the need to internationalize
the Black condition in the United States helped me in my later
choices to become directly involved with the African liberation
struggle.

However, it was Malcolm's personal demeanor: his intelligence, self-discipline, study habits, seriousness, respect for
family, political and cultural awareness, frugality, honesty,
strength in the face of evil fire, work ethic, boldness, humility,
trustworthiness, preparedness, selflessness, and most of all,
winning attitude and integrity that attracted me to him and his
ideas. Most importantly, he came from the same streets I came
from and did not remain a victim. ✗ *Malcolm*

It was Malcolm's influence and his practice of Islam that
helped to push me to visit Africa in 1969 to see the religion in
practice and to see how it served our people at the "source."
Three weeks among Africans who viewed Islam as blood and
oxygen itself was not enough to convert me, but my investiga-

tions in Africa (multiple visits) and continuing study of Islam and other world religions have helped to prepare me to be the man I am today. The spiritual core that Islam embraces—along with all great religions—is that of the moral and ethical person, the good, giving, and serving individual. The selfless individual in the midst of secular corruption crying against hellish odds to return the masses of people to Allah, to good work, and good life is what Malcolm X was about. However, he never lost his Black political and cultural mindset; he expanded.

Deep in the pit of my stomach, I know that when Malcolm broke with the Nation of Islam he also signed his death certificate. He could have had a life with his wife and children, an honored position in international struggle, and a materially comfortable life if he had remained silent. However, there is something inside men and women of honest conscience that will not allow them to take the easy and safe compromise. There is something about being able to live with one's self and daily look spouse, children, family, friends, and co-workers in the face and tell them lie after lie after lie. For Malcolm there was always the question of moral authenticity, the going sub-surface to live one's words, always an honest search.

The principles, values, ideas, and the Islamic life-style that Malcolm was taught and that he taught others was more than foundational theory; they were life itself. The source was the *Holy Koran*—the book that represents each Muslim's personal connection to Allah and his prophet Muhammad. Far from being a perfect man, Malcolm X was a man seeking perfection. His separation from the NOI marked a period of rapid reformation, growth, and much mental pain for Malcolm. In choosing the truth, he assigned his loyalty to a higher power (as he was taught). In doing so, he came up against all the fury and anger of the most military-minded and organized group of Black men in America at that time. Malcolm X understood the gravity of his decision. From that day on, he knew that his time was limited. He had trained many of the men himself. He knew that to speak ill against Elijah Muhammad, the "father," was, in their eyes—regardless of the truth—blasphemy.

Malcolm X's assassination on 21 February 1965 sent young brothers like myself (I was 22) back to tears and weapons. His assassination stopped an important part of the movement. Many in the Black Nationalist community separated themselves from the NOI and refused to even buy their newspaper. We could not prove it, but we knew deep in our hearts that Malcolm was murdered by members of the NOI. It was just as clear to us that the FBI and other law enforcement agencies also carry the blood of Malcolm on their hands.

I

In 1977, I, along with Abena Joan Brown, was working with the North American Zone of FESTAC* in Lagos, Nigeria. I was in charge of making sure that the artists we brought from the Midwest were comfortable and had adequate living quarters. One evening, Stevie Wonder visited our compound. In his entourage was a light-skinned man about ten years my senior, with a close natural and a day-old beard on his face. He was dressed rather casually and had a quick and warm smile. He introduced himself as Louis Farrakhan.

In 1977, the Nation of Islam as we knew it was in a state of flux and confusion. Several factions existed with various

---

*The Second World Black and African Festival of Arts and Culture, January 15 through February 12, 1977.

former members claiming the "seat" of the "father." Farrakhan had originally followed the late Elijah Muhammad's son, Wallace Dean Muhammad, who had directed his followers into mainstream Islamic belief under the name of the World Community of Al-Islam in the West, which later became the American Muslim Mission. Farrakhan's association with W. D. Muhammad was short-lived because of philosophical and religious differences. Prior to my meeting with Farrakhan in Nigeria, I had little reason to think about him.

In the fall of 1977 after returning from Nigeria, Ibrahim Muhammad visited me on behalf of Minister Louis Farrakhan. Ibrahim Muhammad was Farrakhan's confidante, bodyguard, driver, and one-man cheering squad. His message to me was that the Minister was bringing the NOI back under the teachings of the Honorable Elijah Muhammad and wanted my help and counsel.

I did not fully understand the request. After the assassination of Malcolm X, I, like thousands of other non-Muslim activists who had supported the NOI with money and political and cultural identification, ceased to view the NOI among the league of progressive organizations. Also, after Elijah Muhammad died in 1975—many believed that he would never die—it was clear to me and millions of other Black folk that the NOI was not the "people's nation." It was a family religion-business run and controlled by Elijah Muhammad. Upon Mr. Muhammad's death, the NOI monies, properties, papers, legal residences, vacation homes, cars, etc., ended up being contested in court. Just about everything was in the name of or legally owned by Mr. Muhammad and his family. Many referred to them as the "royal family." Once the monies and properties were distributed, they did not stay within the "people's nation" but were distributed among Elijah Muhammad's family, friends, and creditors.

Shortly after Ibrahim Muhammad and I talked, I received a visit from Minister Abdul Farrakhan. Louis Farrakhan had changed his name. However, the suit and the bow tie of the NOI hung on him like the message he was bringing. He was clean-shaven, but still wore his hair in a neatly cut short natural style with very little oil in it. In a very quiet and unassuming manner, Minister Farrakhan shared with me his vision of the new Nation of Islam. He respectfully talked about the differences between himself and Wallace Muhammad and declared that it was his duty to keep the good works of Elijah Muhammad alive. He stated that he felt he could avoid the mistakes of the "father" by not being so exclusive and secretive. His goal was to involve the "Nation" with the larger Black community. His vision, as articulated that fall morning, was much in line with that of many in Chicago's Black political and cultural community.

Farrakhan asked for my help in connecting with the Black Nationalist-activist community in Chicago. I listened carefully, but did not make a commitment. I told him that I would think about his request and get back to him. My first concern was, why did he come to me? I was not a Black leader, I did not have a following, nor did I want one. Yes, I was a published poet-writer and the initiator and co-builder of several independent Black institutions. The Institute of Positive Education, of which I was the director, was/is one of the few independent Black resource centers in the country, at that time, that regularly programmed political and cultural activities.

II.

As a result of Abdul (Louis) Farrakhan's request, I talked to several elder political men and women (who will remain nameless for this essay). Upon their advice, I then contacted about fifty political and cultural activists in Chicago to see if they were willing to meet privately with Farrakhan. Approximately twenty-seven of them—women and men—agreed to attend the meeting. The twenty-seven or so men and women represented some of the major political-cultural activists in Chicago. They came from all key disciplines—education, politics, broadcasting, print media, entertainment, community-based organizations, etc. Their acceptance of my invitation was an indication of how seriously they viewed Minister Farrakhan's request.

Due to the internal "warfare" being waged between the various "Black Muslim" factions at that time, I did something I had never done before with outside groups—we met in the basement of my home. At our first meeting (there were to be several), we listened carefully to the ideas, plans and vision of Minister Abdul (Louis) Farrakhan. By this time he was beginning to surround himself with members of the old NOI. Two of the brothers with him were from outside of Chicago. His words to our group were the same as the ones he shared with me. He spoke clearly, softly, interspersing his comments with remarks about the errors he and others had made in the past. His major point was that this was going to be a new NOI: more political, more involved in the larger Black community, less self-righteous and all-knowing, one that would keep its communication lines open and that would work as part of a Black united front. He stated that the new NOI would follow the teachings of Elijah Muhammad, but would be more creative and insightful in its interpretation of Islam in relationship to the Black community.

After about an hour of listening to Farrakhan's ideas, we turned to our questions. The first question to hit the floor was, "What was his—Louis Farrakhan's—involvement in or connection to the assassination of Malcolm X?" His answer, one that few of us will forget was given in a voice and tone of complete sorrow and resignation. He was obviously prepared for the question. He talked of the history and his personal connection to Malcolm, whom he described as his big brother-teacher and as the man who helped to prepare him. He also talked about Eman Wallace D. Muhammad and his difficulties with him. The core of his remarks was that he may have helped to create the climate, but he neither directly or indirectly had a hand in the assassination of Malcolm X. He also made the following remarks, which were later published in an interview in Black Books Bulletin (Vol. 6, Spring 1978):

> The effects of the changes within the World Community of Islam, in addition to the information I gained about our people in my travels abroad, caused me to reassess the Honorable Elijah Muhammad, his teaching and program for Black people. My articulation of this caused Eman W. D. Muhammad to announce that I was no longer a person with whom the Muslims (WCIW) should associate, listen to or even be given the Muslim greeting. I naturally took this to mean that I was excommunicated from the World Community of Islam.

> Yes. Malcolm as you know was Elijah Muhammad's national representative and spokesman. He was articulate, popular, and his popularity created jealousy and envy among some of the top officials within the movement which resulted in severe problems for him. More importantly, Malcolm saw in the Honorable Elijah Muhammad, what from his perspective, were serious contradictions and Mal-

colm left the Nation or was put out. These are the external similarities between Malcolm and me. Malcolm, in his anger and bitterness, however, made what in my judgement, was a tragic mistake which was to sling mud at his former teacher. This lit the fuse in the highly incendiary atmosphere creating the conditions which allowed Malcolm to be assassinated.

I am not bitter with W. D. Muhammad or the members of the WCIW. In my return to the message and program of the Honorable Elijah Muhammad, and Malcolm going completely away from his teaching and program, lie the internal differences between us.

Minister Farrakhan also focused on the political climate of the time. He talked about the controversy surrounding President John F. Kennedy's death and Malcolm's remarks about it. It was a time of political combustion in and outside of the NOI, he claimed, and many mistakes were made (he emphasized this point). He made it clear that although he had helped to create the climate of violence against Malcolm, he had no personal involvement in the assassination. Further, he had nothing to do with giving the orders for Malcolm's assassination. His explanation, coupled with his formidable persuasive powers, put most of our minds to rest on that question. We agreed, as a group, to meet with him again. We met amongst ourselves and agreed that Minister Farrakhan had told us the truth. We agreed to put forth some effort on his behalf with a deep understanding that much of his work was going to be focused on the problems facing the entire Black community and that some of us would be his outside advisors.

The group, we never named ourselves, organized into committees and began to orchestrate the "official" coming out of Minister Farrakhan. Our committees consisted of security, publicity, public-speaking, etc. We pooled our monies and went to work. This was a completely volunteer group of seasoned men and women who believed Farrakhan when he stated that he did not have any involvement in the death of Malcolm X, and that he was not attempting to build another Muslim religious organization that separated itself from the larger Black community. His stated goal was to work with all Black people regardless of religious, political, or philosophical leanings. We believed him. We worked hard have him interviewed by key newspapers and journals. We scheduled his first talk to the community for November 15, 1977 at the Institute of Positive Education. The atmosphere inside the building on the night of his talk was electric. The school's auditorium was packed; people standing in the aisles and outside in the streets. These were the early days, his new beginnings: no Fruit of Islam, no hand searches of our people prior to his talk, and he was a hit.

For the next three to six months, the NOI, still in its rebuilding process, met weekly at the Institute of Positive Education (we charged them ninety-nine dollars a week). For close to a year we worked together. By the fall of 1978, many of the old-line NOI members were coming back, and I and others could see that Minister Farrakhan was definitely going in the same direction as his teacher Elijah Muhammad. His number-two man, Ibrahim Muhammad, left. I and the group that helped him distanced ourselves. We tired rather quickly of being invited to share the dais while Farrakhan gave *the* word for three hours each Saviour's Day.

III

There is much that I'm leaving out of this. However, I will state that two people whom I love warned me to be careful in my dealings with Farrakhan. Betty Shabazz, Malcolm X's widow, with whom I shared a flight to New York in February 1979, suggested strongly that I not turn my back on Minister Farrakhan, and, if I had not already done so, not to get too close. Just before his death, one of the members of the group that earlier met with Farrakhan, Dr. Bobby Wright, also suggested strongly that I distance myself. During my first year of contact with Minister Farrakhan (1977-1978), he and I spoke frequently. After that, my contact with him and the NOI was seldom. When such contacts did occur, they were generally arranged by his representative requesting my presence at a public function. Since 1979, I've only spoken to the now Honorable Louis Farrakhan once.

I write this essay principally because my history in this regard needs to be on record and the central question about Minister Farrakhan's involvement in the death of Malcolm X has again entered our conscience and public debate. Regardless of my personal relationship to Minister Farrakhan, it is a fact that he is a leader who cannot, and should not, be dismissed or minimized by the assessment of others outside of the Black community who have ulterior motives. However, his last seventeen years of rebuilding have not insulated him from the unanswered questions. That these questions are being revisited by the white press is something that we must be mindful of because their hatred of the NOI and Minister Farrakhan is also well-documented.

According to the *Baltimore Sun* (March 12, 1994),

> five prominent black ministers have accused Nation of Islam leader Louis Farrakhan of hypocrisy for preaching against black-on-black violence while failing to condemn crimes allegedly linked to his organization.

The five ministers who issued an open letter to Minister Farrakhan included Reverend Eugene Rivers, whose father was a Black Muslim who worked with both Malcolm X and Minister Farrakhan. The clergymen, from Boston and Cambridge, Massachusetts, "charged that Nation of Islam members have been accused of or connected to involvement in several brutal attacks on blacks, including the 1965 assassination of black leader Malcolm X." They go on to publicly ask the question,

> Given that five members of the Newark mosque were identified as Malcolm's killers by one of the assassins and that you [Farrakhan] were reportedly at the Newark mosque in the day of Malcolm's assassination, what responsibility do you bear for this heinous example of black-on-black violence?

Further concerns are raised in documentary film by Jack Baxter and Jefri Muhammad, which shows Farrakhan in a February 1993 speech to followers claiming that the Nation of Islam killed Malcolm X for being a "traitor."

An additional revelation is that Betty Shabazz, Malcolm X's widow, has now publicly stated, without ambiguity, that Farrakhan was directly involved in the death of her husband. On the Gabe Pressman Show, aired 13 March 1994, she was asked by Gabe Pressman*, "Do you think that Louis Farrakhan had anything to do with the death of your husband?" Her response was, "Of course, yes... Nobody kept it a secret. It was a badge of honor. Everybody talked about it. Yes." To my knowledge, this was the first time that Betty Shabazz ever publicly connected Farrakhan to her husband's assassination.

---

* This interview is self-serving. During Malcolm's life I'm told that Mr. Pressman was a critic.

Who among us, if we are honest and sincere in our search, can forget the words spoken by Minister Farrakhan on Saviour's Day, March 29, 1993:

> Every prophet had a community of zealots that, when you rose up against that prophet, the people would rise up and kill you. That person could be a doorman, a sweeper, a blind person—doesn't make any difference. When you hurt the prophet, the people say, "You must die."

> The Honorable Elijah Muhammad didn't have to give order to kill anybody; we already were ordered to kill anybody by the love of that man who gave us life. I'm not a killer, but when you mess with that man, I become that because that's the man that [sic] gave me life. The Hon. Elijah Muhammad taught me all I know...in order that I could produce children of consequence.

> If you want to live, you leave that man alone where we are concerned. When Malcolm stepped across that line, death was inevitable.

My final concern is the lack of open and honest criticism of Minister Farrakhan and the NOI from those of us who helped him to rise again. I, too, am guilty of this. Indeed, I have tried to call and meet with Minister Farrakhan; I have raised my voice privately at Black meetings and gatherings but not in a detailed criticism of the NOI since its rise in 1977. However, on Sunday, 18 July 1993, the *Chicago Sun Times* published a major interview and story on Minister Farrakhan by Mary A. Johnson. I was interviewed for the article and made several brief remarks, which were incorporated into the article as follows:

> Haki Madhubuti, founder of the Third World Press and a pioneer in the black arts community, said Farrakhan has made great strides in spreading his religion and self-reliance message to blacks in prison and also has tremendous influence among young black men.

But Madhubuti urges careful scrutiny. "I would hope that people would look at his programs as well as anybody else's programs with a very, very critical eye," he said. "Black people have been disappointed so much and our needs are so great that we need a leadership that truly loves our community."

Twice, I have been called on regarding my relationship to Minister Farrakhan by his national spokesman, Khalid Abdul Muhammad. Following the publication of this article, Muhammad again approached me at a National Black Male Conference at Southern University at Baton Rouge in the summer of 1993. He wanted to know why I was talking to the "white man" about the minister. I answered, "I talked to the same Black reporter that Minister Farrakhan talked to. She is trusted and fair in her reportage on our community. Are you suggesting that Farrakhan is beyond criticism?" He responded with continued criticism of me, and I had to cut him short because I had to give a major speech in less than a half an hour. We parted with my stating that he obviously misread the article and that Minister Farrakhan was his leader and not mine.

The next evening in a public address in New Orleans, Khalid Muhammad criticized those Blacks he did not agree with. He called me out specifically in regards to my remarks quoted in the *Chicago Sun-Times*:

Some of you heard on the news that the skinheads had put the Honorable Louis Farrakhan as public enemy number one on their hit list. Well, I think we need to pay the skinheads a visit. We should bum rush them. Black boot stomp their doors down and beat the hell out of every skinhead we can find and put our foot in their behinds everywhere we can find one just for the thought of attacking Louis Farrakhan, just for the thought of doing it.

And these bootlicking Negroes. I understand that Haki Madhubuti, as much respect as I have for him, sent a veiled

> criticism at the Honorable Louis Farrakhan in the *Chicago Times* [sic]. Lu Palmer and some of these other bootlicking Negroes. Well we're tired and sick and tired of all these attacks that are coming against God's messenger and man in our midst today. And we say today that you're either going to start saying something good about Louis Farrakhan or you ain't gonna say nothing about him at all. You'll just keep his name out of your mouth.

For the National Spokesman of the Nation of Islam to group the thoughts and actions of Lu Palmer and myself with the skinheads is very dangerous and demonstrates how far beyond reality such uncritical thinking goes. Lu Palmer is without question one of our great elders who has given his life to our struggle. It is clear to activists in Chicago that Harold Washington became mayor largely because of the early work of Lu Palmer and others.

Where Is This Going?

After thirty years in Black struggle, have we come to the point where I/we have to fear our own "Black" brothers? If this is the case, what is the role of the critical thinkers among us? Do we too lock-step to the ideas that run counter to our own existence and future?

Some suggestions and observations:

1. The coalition founded in 1993 between the top Black human rights organizations, Black politicians, and the NOI was not only on time, it was long overdue. It is imperative that Minister Louis Farrakhan be included in the upcoming African American leadership summit and any other national think tanks discussing the future of Black folks.

2. The NOI needs to stop reacting to the Anti-Defamation

League (ADL) and other Jewish organizations. The ADL, with its own dubious reputation, is only doing what it sees as in its best interest, politically and financially. The ADL is on the attack, and Farrakhan and the NOI—due to some serious linguistic, communication and historical errors, represent a formidable foe at the national level, mainly in the arena of public relations. That much of this battle is a religious war as much as a political one is lost in much of the verbiage. The Judaic/Islamic confrontation that is waged each day in the Middle East is partially the source of the problem here. The fact that the Jewish ADL and the Muslim NOI are embroiled in a "religious" war of words is somehow forgotten and/or not highlighted in the current debate.

3. Do not expect the ADL or other like-minded Jewish organizations to forget their history or pain and engage in meaningful dialogue. Mr. Farrakhan has tried to reach out to local and national Jewish representatives in music and dialogue. Some of this worked. However there are powerful forces in the Jewish community that do not want this problem to go away for any number of reasons, including:

    a. Many Jews are racist and hide behind their people's suffering as a badge of "honor." Due to their own holocaust (a historical fact) and the oppression that they endure even today, many Jews feel that they are beyond criticism. Therefore, any questions about the Jewish worldview in its relationship to the Palestinians, South Africa, or Jewish involvement with African Americans are not answered. The questions are considered anti-Semitic by many.

b.   European American Jews are white too. Most do not deny this. A great many daily try to stay white by marrying other white ethnics and running from "Jewish" identity at the same level many Blacks try to run from any African connection. Most Blacks see Jews as white and seldom separate them from their white brothers and sisters of other cultural groups.

c.   Many Jews are *genuinely* hurt as a result of all the controversy because they deeply love Black culture. Many of their lives have been transformed and enriched as a result of Black people and our culture. Some of this hurt borders on disbelief and is translated into anger directed at Farrakhan and the NOI. He is a high-profile leader and makes excellent copy on any day.

d.   Jewish media is also white media. Most people know that *Commentary* is a Jewish-owned journal, but few are aware of the Jewish and part-Jewish ownership of the *New York Times*, the *Washington Post*, the *New Republic*, etc. The Jewish influence in directing the public discourse in reference to their struggle is nothing less than masterful. This does not necessarily imply total ownership, it implies skill and sophistication, organization and, yes, influence.

4.   Khalid Abdul Muhammad and other ministers of the NOI, in their public pronouncements, must observe some critical standards of political discourse. It is easy to sell "wolf tickets"—it is a tradition in the Black community. To talk badly about white folks is not the art it used to be. Many of us can do it rather well. However, I have yet to hear of any Blacks organizing to desecrate Jewish cemeteries or synagogues, take Jewish lives, or prohibit them from

acquiring the best education or advancing in their chosen profession. Our challenge is to articulate to our people, especially young people, a developmental message. Very seldom can any people sustain a movement or build a nation on an antiwhite, anticapitalist, antidemocratic or antireligious message. Young students are impressionable and we adults, and I use that word cautiously, must be responsible in our communication and interactions with them. Communicate to them what we stand for in detail, not slogans and breastbeating. To his credit, in the 16 February 1994 issue of the *Final Call,* the NOI's official publication and monthly newspaper, Minister Louis Farrakhan takes Minister Khalid A. Muhammad to task in a rather detailed editorial:

> I have warned Brother Khalid several times about his manner of representing the truths. I have told him that he is not representing himself and that one day, if he is not careful, he might find himself clashing with me in the public and that this would not serve our best interest or the interests of our people, but would serve the interest of our enemies.

5. This continued "Black-Jewish battle," which is in reality a battle between *some* Blacks and *some* Jews, is not a national problem. However, focusing on it takes us away from the real and critical problems confronting Blacks every day. The deep and unrelenting crises in education, health care, housing, and employment that we face locally, nationally and internationally take a back seat to this name-calling. What is our position on GATT and NAFTA? How do we help South Africans move toward Black rule? How do we stop any of the eight wars now waging in Africa? What do we do about the eight hundred thousand

Black men and fifty thousand Black women locked up in American prisons? What about the homeless, helpless, and hopeless among us? Where is our political and economic plan for the twenty-first century?

6. Minister Farrakhan and his representatives need to leave the memory of Malcolm X alone. Let him rest in peace. He is truly honored among our people and the NOI will lose this battle if it persists. Also, Minister Farrakhan must, in a detailed and honest manner, answer the questions about his involvement or noninvolvement in the assassination of Malcolm X. This question will not go away and the raising of it cannot be dismissed as a Jewish plot against him.

7. Most Blacks are not willing to buy into new dogmas, either religious or secular. Most realize that any form of absolutism stops development and that religious fundamentalism, whether Islamic, Christian, Jewish (yes, there are Black Jews—Hebrews), runs counter to ally-building in the Black world. Xenophobia and racial and religious bigotry have been used throughout history to denigrate the African world. We must not duplicate such efforts.

8. We need uncompromising leadership. However, we do not need leadership that is untouchable or unfathomable. We do not need self-righteous leadership that is more concerned with being *the* leader than with serving the people. We are living in a very difficult time of fragmentation and destruction. We need wise and serious women and men willing to take the liberating leap beyond their own egos to embrace a plan of action that will take into account the lives of not only Black people, but the world's

people. Among some Black leaders, the boundaries of separation between the people and themselves has reached "guru" status. This is very dangerous because common folks represent a vital segment of reality, and the more a leader is closeted or cloistered among a select group of "yes" people or noncritical co-workers and believers, the more remote the chances that new knowledge will be available to inform his or her decisions. Taking on a revered persona is a serious trap that Black leadership must avoid. According to Kramer and Alstad in *The Guru Papers*, it is symptomatic of authoritarian power:

> Being a "knower" as opposed to a seeker, is part of being a guru. This implies an essential division between the guru and others. The guru in effect says "I'm here, and you're there; and not only can I help you move from here to there, but that's what I'm here for." Being different (or, rather, being perceived as different) is the foundation of the guru's dominance. Relations of dominance and submission often contain extreme emotions. But if dominance and submission are the essential ingredients in the glue holding the bond together, the connection is not really personal. Gurus and disciple need each other, but as roles, not as individuals, which makes real human connection almost impossible. So gurus must create other ways of turning themselves on beside intimacy, the most usual being adulation, material wealth, and impersonal sexuality and power.

9.   Black leadership needs to be expanded. What about Black professional organizations, the National Baptist Convention (12 million members), Black fraternities and sororities, and most importantly, Blacks in finance and business? We need to use all of our talent. The NOI has to be kept in perspective. Its active membership is not as large as many Black churches. Any Sunday in most Black urban centers, you can find a single Black church serving 5 to

15,000 worshippers. The Progressive Baptist Convention is comprised of about 7 million members. Without a doubt, the strongest institution in the Black community is the church. The largest "political" organization is the National Association for the Advancement of Colored People (NAACP) with a membership of 650,000.

10. What about the questions that Farrakhan and the spokespersons of the NOI *are* asking of America on behalf of Black people. Rather than receiving answers, they get attacks, which has been an effective way of avoiding the questions. What about reparations for Black people? Are any of the questions asked of Jewish people legitimate? What about the Palestinian question? What about Israel's involvement with the white South African government in the areas of security and military readiness? What about the representation of Black athletes by Jewish lawyers? What about the Jewish influence in Hollywood? Will the current crop of Black leadership ask the same kind of questions that Farrakhan has?

Farrakhan is caught between responding to his own questions or responding to the attacks made on the questions asked. The flood of negative criticism that he has received has forced many Blacks into noncritical support of him because they view the attacks as unfair and way out of proportion to the questions. Which is true. (This is by no means to negate any anti-Jewish comments voiced by Farrakhan or his representatives.) Therefore, even when Malcolm's widow, Dr. Shabazz, asks a key question or states her belief around the question she is questioned by Blacks as to her motives for voicing her concerns, as if she is incorrect for questioning. This is crazy! The political climate that is currently operating in reference to Minister Farrakhan is one created by the white and Jewish media. Therefore, thinking Blacks who have serious and critical questions of him must now be quiet or be perceived as being in bed with the "white man." Oppression makes people think and act in silly ways.

However, my brother Farrakhan, just because you are under attack does not make you completely right. Just because you are Black and male does not relieve you from the responsibility of sticking to the facts and facts alone when making political and cultural points. Just because you are strong and will not bend down or be silent does not mean that you have not or will not make mistakes. Just because you have a history of struggle on behalf of the Black community does not mean that you have not prospered as a result of our struggle. Finally, just because you are a spiritual leader, does not mean that the only person or entity who can assess your work is God/Allah. We, the people, and, yes, your peers, have that right also. As long as you speak in the name of Black people as their/our representative, you must listen to us. When you are under fire, we feel the heat.

As one who aided Minister Louis Farrakhan at great risk and expense in the beginning, I now ask that he consider these suggestions seriously. One of the recommendations suggested by the group who met with Farrakhan in 1977 was the establishment of an outside council of elders to advise him. I think that this idea should be reconsidered. Additionally, Farrakhan should consider issuing a statement in the *Final Call* that would address the key questions raised by his friends and his enemies.

We will indeed cross this sea of sharks; however, it is not a lifeboat that we need. We need expertly run ships with a home port in tune with the best that the Black African world has to offer.

CLARENCE THOMAS

The Best White Man for the Job?

I think that much of the comments and criticism that surrounded Clarence Thomas' nomination to the Supreme Court have missed the point: *America works*. One does not have to be an historian to realize that the social engineering and the melting-pot theories of the last one hundred years or so have produced literally millions of Black men and women who think, act, and perceive the world and the future the same as Clarence Thomas.

To believe that a Black conservative is an oddity is to deny reality. Most African Americans would rather work than receive handouts, be admitted to college on merit rather than special programs, be employed because of their skills rather than skin pigmentation, be involved in politics—not as a Democrat or Republican—but as a free, thinking independent. Most Black people are aware of the importance and absolute necessity of family, spiritual living, and "free enterprise" in the maintenance, maturation, stability, and growth of their community, people and nation. Clarence Thomas is not an exception in his "bootstrap" philosophy. The great majority of Black folk who have made their presence known in America have worked hard and overtime. If such beliefs are defined as conservative, well, include me.

However, this is the United States. Africans did not arrive

here by travelling first-class on the Mayflower or walking on the water. Europeans skillfully, with the aid of some Africans, raped Africa of its best and brightest and literally sprinkled Black people around the world. Today, there are over sixty-five million people of African descent in Brazil, another forty million or more in South America, and approximately thirty-five million in the United States. And, the great tragedy of these enslaved Africans in the Western world is that most are unaware of their continued "enslavement," and there is little, if any, communication between us.

This brings me to the question of race. Taylor Branch, in his book *Parting the Waters*, a massive study of the life of Martin Luther King, Jr. and the Civil Rights struggle, states, "almost as color defines vision itself, race shapes the cultural eye—what we do not notice, the reach of empathy and the alignment of response. This subliminal force recommends care in choosing a point of view for a history grounded in race." The white response to the majority of the world's people, who are not white, is indeed grounded in race. More than any other factor in the Eurocentric context, race defines, categorizes, tracks, destroys, and redefines cultures. The color question in America has a way of driving most people into silliness and/or madness.

The white process of "seasoning" or acculturation of most Black folk in America has been very effective. Clarence Thomas is the latest and most glaring example of a fully home-grown, created negro in the grand tradition of the Republic. This system of white supremacy that we live under is very efficient in the brain mismanagement of a whole lot of people: Black, White, Yellow, Brown, and Red. That Clarence Tho-

mas is against affirmative action, abortion, quotas in employment and education, and civil rights legislation to aid the
oppressed is quite understandable. Remember, we all do what
we have been taught to do. He has given big credit to white
people for his education, and it is clear that his undergraduate
and law degrees (which are in white studies) have fully prepared him to work in the best interests of his teachers and
against the interests and intentions of Black people and other
people of color. Thomas' white or Eurocentric philosophy is
not unusual. Millions of Black people who have been, as they
put it, "trapped in a Black body" function daily at an uncon-
scious level with a white mind and worldview. Their self-
hatred translates hourly into many personal or professional acts
that they hope will endear them to the very people who have
done them the greatest harm: white people. Clarence Thomas
is a Black man who thinks and acts like a white man in both his
personal and professional life.

The long-lasting and debilitating effects of "white studies"
on the psyche of Black people is undeniable. From the studies
of Franz Fanon and Bobby Wright to that of Frances Cress
Welsing, Wade Nobles, Cheikh Anta Diop, and Chancellor
Williams, it is clear that many white people have gone to great
lengths to acquire the uncompromising allegiance and love of
Black folk.

The Supreme Court is the last voice on the legal landscape
in this country. To have Clarence Thomas serve on it is of
immense importance. The argument regarding whether or not
he is qualified for the position is moot. His confirmation may
actually be a blessing in disguise for African American people
in that his actions on the court will send a signal to all Americas

that Black folk are not homogeneous in thought and lifestyle. His inclusion demonstrates that there are many Blacks in this country who are alive, well, and grinning to do the bidding and dirty work of white people if provided with the correct incentives (handouts).

As a Supreme Court Justice will Clarence Thomas vote as if he is a brother from another planet? If his history is to be believed, he will be consistent with his vote. However, on the Supreme Court and all other courts of this land, what separate Clarence Thomas and other judges is color. The major difference between conservative Thomas and white conservative judges is that he may remember that in the beginning of his life he was called "nigger" to his face. Justice Clarence Thomas, as was the case in the lower court, will still be called nigger, but not to his face. Although color still rules the landscape in America, Justice Thomas will follow the conservative majority in his contribution.

Post-Script

The picture that I remember the clearest of Clarence Thomas is that of him standing next to then-President Bush as his nomination was announced to the press: Clarence Thomas, with head bowed and right hand to lips, obviously fighting back the tears, this Black man, plump and shorter than Bush, seemed much darker contrasted to Bush's pale whiteness. This picture is one of gratefulness, of undying surrender, of supreme commitment to the ideas, positions, and worldview of Mr. Bush and men like him. They know, deep in the reserves of their minds, that Clarence would not fail them. They were right!

A review of Justice Thomas voting record over the last two

years put him squarely in the camp of conservative justices William H. Rehnquist, Anthony M. Kennedy, and Atonin Scalia. Justice Thomas has voted against Black folks and other people of color every time in the five major cases involving civil rights and civil liberties.

According to United States Supreme Court records, he voted with the conservative majority in (1) *Presley vs. Etowah County* (1992), which stripped budgetary authority from the first Black commissioner elected in that county since Reconstruction, thereby making the position irrelevant; (2) *Hudson vs. McMillan* (1992), in which Thomas, voting with Justice Scalia (the most conservative of all justices), voted against the majority which ruled that the severe beating by guards in a Louisiana prison of an inmate who was "hog-tied" on the floor was a violation of the Eighth Amendment against cruel and inhuman punishment; (3) *St. Mary's Honor Center vs. Hicks* (1993), in which Thomas was the deciding vote against an employee who proved that his employer had lied in a job-bias claim; and (4) *Shaw vs. Reno* (1993), in which Thomas was again the deciding vote in a case that highlights the social division between Blacks and whites in North Carolina. In this last case, on 29 July 29 1993, the eight white justices were equally divided over the issue of "positive gerrymandering" in two North Carolina congressional districts to allow two Blacks to be elected to Congress. After 125 years of white gerrymandering to maintaining white power, the mainly white North Carolina legislature, used the 1990 census and redistricting tactics to create two Black-majority districts. The Republican Party and others went to court claiming that such an act violated the rights of white people. Thomas' vote was the deciding hammer in the political aspirations of North Carolina Blacks who have not had representation since the last century. In another case, (5) *Sale vs. Haitian Centers Council* (1993), the court's decision virtually closed the doors of the United States to Black Haitians fleeing an oppressive government seeking political asylum. Under this ruling, Haitians picked up on the oceans can be returned to Haiti without due process.

After the belittling spectacle of the Anita Hill/Clarence Thomas soap opera, few would have thought that Thomas could top that. Well, welcome to Part II of the "Amos and Andy Show." However, there is little that is funny here: Justice Thomas does not scratch his head in public, and when he smiles or laughs, he does so in Yale-like silences observing the protocols of his education and the mightiest court in the land.

HAITI

(for the Haitian people and Randall Robinson)

in haiti at wahoo bay beach of port-au-prince
there are beautiful women in bathing suits
with men who are young, light-skinned and rich.
you are welcomed if you run with the right wolves.

in port-au-prince, on the other side of the water
fenced off from wahoo bay beach
a few children receive 19th century education in
one room shanties without running water or toilets.
their parents cook on outdoor woodfires and
pass waste in secret spots or community latrines.
they live in poverty within poverty and they elected a
priest to represent their dreams.
he promised food, clean water, education, wood, seeds,
       fairness, democracy and peace on earth.

the people of haiti are angry with u.s. presidents.
the haitian military forced their elected priest to flee in the
night, with their dreams and prayers
in a quickly packed suitcase.

the people are uneducated, not stupid.
democracy is coming to south africa and
haiti drowns in white promises.

bill clinton talks in codes as
paramilitary terror squads beat patriotism into the people.
american businesses pay 14 cents an hour to the peasants
and
provide japanese toys and airline tickets to the elite.

the people of haiti are angry with u.s. presidents.
they take boat rides by the thousands
to cross a sea made of their dead for america.
most are returned on military ships,
unsuitable as political refugees.
we are told that race is not the problem
it is the island, its not cuba.

the rich in haiti diet,
the poor starve and disappear if they complain too loudly.
randall robinson lived on water and tomato juice
his eyes sank into his forehead for a month.
his eyes are clear and so is he.

the new duvalierists rule a dirty capital,
when rain comes the people join the mud,
the rich drive jeeps made in the U.S.A.
the "MREs" —morally repugnant elite are like elite
everywhere:
they do not feel for others,
they hide their eyes,
they wear foreign made clothes,
their children have private playgrounds and educations,
they live on hills and laugh at the dark people who don't
even own the night.
they speak the language of killers.

the rich do not fear elected priests or ignorant peasants,
they have good uncles across the water,
currently he is grayish blond,
has a smooth southern accent,
and talks real fast from both sides of his mouth
before him
a transplanted texan played cowboy on the high seas
before him
a californian with an excellent make-up man
yawned whenever haiti was mentioned
before him...

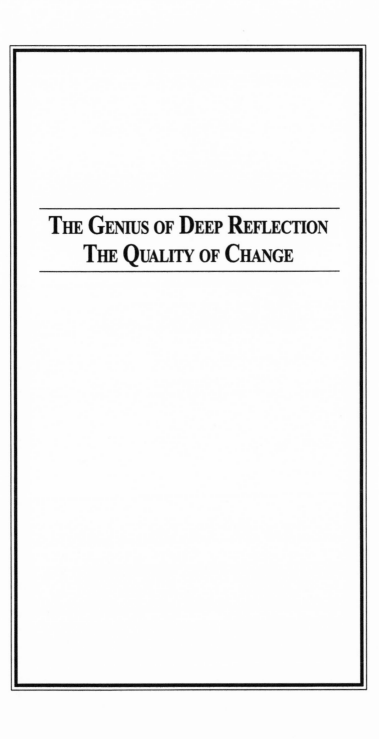

THE GENIUS OF DEEP REFLECTION
THE QUALITY OF CHANGE

RAPE: THE MALE CRIME

On Becoming Anti-Rapist

There are mobs & strangers
in us
who scream of the women
wanted and
will get
as if the women are ours for the
taking.

In 1991, the crime of rape in the United States entered our consciousness with a force equivalent to our discovery of the dissolution of the U.S.S.R. The trials of William Kennedy Smith (of the "Camelot" family) and "Iron" Mike Tyson (former heavyweight boxing champion of the entire world) shared the front pages and provided talk show hosts with subject matter on a topic that is usually confined to women's groups and the butt jokes of many men. Since women comprise over fifty percent of the world's population and a clear majority in this country, one would think that the question of rape would not still be hidden in the "minor concerns" files of men.

However, what is not hidden is that Mr. Kennedy Smith and Mr. Tyson both tried defenses that blamed the women in question. For Smith, that tactic was successful; for Tyson, it failed. Pages of analysis have been written on both cases and

I do not wish to add to them. One can safely state that no woman wants to be raped And if men were raped as frequently as women are, rape would be a federal crime rivaling that of murder and bank robbery. If car-jacking can command federal attention, why are we still treating rape as if it is a "boys will be boys" sport or a "woman's problem" (as in "blame the victim")? In the great majority of the sex crimes against women in the United States, the women are put on trial as if they planned and executed their own rapes.

Male acculturation (more accurately, male "seasoning,") is anti-female, anti-womanist/feminist, and anti-reason when it comes to women's equal measure and place in society. This flawed socialization of men is not confined to the West but permeates most, if not all, cultures in the modern world. Most men have been taught to treat, respond, listen, and react to women from a male's point of view. Black men are not an exception here. We, too, are imprisoned with an intellectual/ spiritual/sexual understanding of women based upon anti- quated male culture and sexist orientation (or miseducation). For example, sex or sexuality is hardly ever discussed, debated, or taught to Black men in a non-threatening or nonembarrassing family or community setting.

Too many men's view of women, specifically Black women outside of their immediate families, is often one of "bitch," "my woman," "ho," or any number of designations that demean and characterize Black women as less than whole and productive persons. Our missteps toward an understanding of women are compounded by the cultural environments where much of the talk about women takes place: street corners, locker rooms, male clubs, sporting events, bars, military bases, business trips, playgrounds, workplaces, basketball courts, etc. Generally, women are not discussed in these settings as intellectual or culturally compatible partners. Rather the discussion focuses on what is the best way to "screw" or control them?

These are, indeed, learning environments that traditionally are not kind to women. The point of view that is affirmed all too often is the ownership of women. Men are taught to see women as commodities and/or objects for men's sexual releases and sexual fantasies; also, most women are considered "inferiors" to men and thus are not to be respected or trusted. Such thinking is encouraged and legitimized by our culture and transmitted via institutional structures (i.e., churches, workplaces), mass media (*i.e., Playboy* and *Penthouse*), misogynist music (rap and mainstream), and R-rated and horror films that use exploitative images of women. And, of course, there are the ever present, tall, trim, "Barbie-doll" women featured in advertising for everything from condoms to the latest diet "cures." Few men have been taught, really taught, from birth—to the heart, to the gut—to respect, value, or even, on occasion, to honor women. Only until very recently has it been confirmed in Western culture that rape (unwelcomed/uninvited sex) is criminal, evil, and antihuman.

our mothers, sisters, wives and
daughters ceased to be the
women men want   we think of them as
loving family   music & soul   bright wonderments.
they are not locker room talk
not the hunted lust or   dirty
cunt burnin hos.
bright wonderments are excluded   by association as

blood & heart   bone & memory
& we will destroy a rapist's knee caps,
& write early grave on his thoughts
to protect them.

Proximity defines human relationships. Exceptions should be noted, but in most cultures and most certainly within the Black/African worldview, family and extended family ties are honored and respected. One's sexual personhood in a healthy culture is nurtured, respected, and protected. In order to get a personal fix here, an understanding of the natural prohibitions against rape, think of your own personhood being violated. Think of your own family being subjected to this act. Think of the enslavement of African people. On most plantations, it was common to have breeding houses where some of our great-great-grandmothers were forced to open their insides for the sick satisfaction of white slave owners, overseers and enslaved Black men. This forced sexual penetration of African women led to the creation of the mixed-race people here and around the world. There is a saying in South Africa that the colored race did not exist until nine months after white men arrived. This demeaning of Black women and other women is amplified in today's culture where it is not uncommon for young men to proclaim that "pussy is a penny a pound." However, we are told that such a statement is not meant for one's own mother, grandmother, sister, daughter, aunt, niece, close relative, or extended family. Yet, the point must be made rather emphatically that incest (family rape) is on the rise in this country. Incest between adults and children is often not revealed until the children are adults. At that point, their lives are so confused and damaged that many continue the incestuous acts.

it will do us large to recall
when the animal in us rises
that all women are someone's
mother, sister wife or daughter
and are not fruit to be stolen when hungry.

Part of the answer is found in the question: Is it possible or realistic to view all women as precious persons? Selective memory plays an important role here. Most men who rape are seriously ill and improperly educated. They do not view women outside of their "protected zone" as precious blood, do not see them as extended human family, and do not see them as individuals or independent persons to be respected as most men respect other men. Mental illness, or brain mismanagement, blocks out reality, shattering and negating respect for self and others, especially those whom one wishes to take advantage of. Power always lurks behind rape. Rape is an act of aggression that asserts power by defaming and defiling. Most men have been taught—either directly or indirectly—to solve problems with force. Such force may be verbal or physical. Violence is the answer that is promoted in media everywhere, from Saturday morning cartoons to everyday television to R-rated films. Popular culture has a way of trivializing reality and confusing human expectations, especially with regard to relationships between men and women. For too many Black people, the popular has been internalized. In many instances, the media define us, including our relationships to each other.

Women have been at the forefront of the anti-rape struggle. Much of this work has taken place in nontraditional employment, such as serving in police and fire departments, as top professors and administrators in higher education, as elected and appointed public servants in politics, and in the fields of medicine and law. However, the most pronounced presence and "advancement" of women has been seen in the military. We are told that the military, in terms of social development remains at the cutting edge of changes—especially in the progress of Blacks and women soldiers. However, according to Gary A. Warner in the *San Francisco Examiner* (30 December 1992), the occurrence of rape against women in the military is far greater than that in civilian life:

> A woman serving in the Army is 50 percent more likely to be raped than a civilian, newly released military records obtained by the Orange County Register show.
>
> From 1987 to 1991, 484 female soldiers were raped while on active duty, according to Department of the Army records released after a Freedom of Information Act request.
>
> The Army rate of 129 rape cases per 100,000 population in 1990 exceeds nationwide statistics for the same year compiled by the FBI of 80 confirmed rape cases per 100,000 women. The 1990 statistics are the latest compatible ones available.

The brutality of everyday life continues to confirm the necessity for caring men and women to confront inhuman acts that cloud and prevent wholesome development. Much of what is defined as sexual "pleasure" today comes at the terrible expense of girls and often boys. To walk Times Square or any number of big-city playgrounds after dark is to view how pervasively the popular, throwaway culture has trapped, corrupted, and sexually abused too many of our children. In the United States the sexual abuse of runaway children, and children sentenced to foster care and poorly supervised orphanages, is nothing less than scandalous. The proliferation of battered women's shelters and the most recent revelation of the sexual abuse of women incarcerated in the nation's prisons only underscores the prevailing view of women by a substantial number of men, as sex objects for whatever sick acts that enter their minds.

Such abuse of children is not confined to the United States. Ron O' Grady, coordinator of the International Campaign to End Child Prostitution in Asiatic Tourism, fights an uphill battle to highlight the physical and economic maltreatment of children. Murray Kempton in his essay, "A New Colonialism" (the *New York Review of Books*, 19 November 1992) reminds us of Thailand's "supermarkets for the purchases of small and disposable bodies." He goes on to state that:

> Tourism is central to Thailand's developmental efforts; and the attractions of its ancient culture compare but meagerly to the compelling pull its brothels exercise upon foreign visitors. The government does its duty to the economy by encouraging houses of prostitution and pays its debt to propriety with its insistence that no more than 10,000 children work there. Private observers concerned with larger matters than the good name of public officials estimate the real total of child prostitutes in Thailand at 200,000....

> The hunters and others of children find no border closed. They have ranged into South China carrying television sets to swap one per child. The peasants who cursed the day a useless girl was born know better now: they can sell her for consumers overseas and be consumers themselves. Traffickers less adventurous stay at home and contrive travel agencies that offer cheap trips to Kuala Lumpur that end up with sexual enslavement in Japan or Malaysia.

That this state of affairs is not better known speaks loudly and clearly to the devaluation of female children. The war in Sarajevo, Bosnia and Herzegovinia again highlights the status of women internationally. In the rush toward "ethnic cleansing" and narrow and exclusive nationalism, Serbian soldiers have been indicted for murder and other war crimes. The story of one such soldier, Borislav Herak, is instructive. According to an article by John F. Burns in the *New York Times* (November 27, 1992) entitled "A Serbian Fighter's Trial of Brutality," Mr. Herak and other soldiers were given the go-ahead to rape and kill Muslim women:

> The indictment lists 29 individual murders between June and October, including eight rape-murders of Muslim women held prisoner in an abandoned motel and cafe outside Vogosca, seven miles north of Sarajevo, where, Mr. Herak said, he and other Serbian fighters were encouraged to rape women and then take them away to kill them in hilltops and other deserted places.

> The indictment also covers the killings of at least 220 other Muslim civilians in which Mr. Herak has confessed to being a witness or taking part, many of them women and children. (Also see the January 4, 1993 issue of *Newsweek.*)

On January 9, 1993, *New York Times'* reporter Alan Riding, in a front page story, reports that an independent European inquiry headed by Dame Anne Warburton, a former British diplomat, found that 20,000 Muslim woman have been raped by Bosnian Serb soldiers. According to the *Times,* this was "a deliberate pattern of abuse aimed at driving them from their houses in Bosnia and Herzegovina."

Much in the lives of women is not music or melody but is their dancing to the beat of the unhealthy and often killing drums of men and male teenagers. Rape is not the fault of women; however, in a male-dominated world, the victims are often put on the defensive and forced to rationalize their gender and their personhood.

Rape is not a reward for warriors
it is war itself

a deep, deep tearing, a dislocating of
the core of the womanself.
rape rips heartlessly
soul from spirit,
obliterating colors from beauty and body
replacing melody and music with
rat venom noise
and uninterrupted intrusion and beatings.

The brutality of rape is universal. Most modern cultures—European, American, African, Asian, religious and secular—grapple with this crime. Rarely is there discussion, and, more often than not, women are discouraged from being a part the debates and edicts. Rape is cross-cultural. I have not visited, heard of, or read about any rape-free societies. The war against women is international. Daily, around the world, women fight for a little dignity and their earned place in the world. And men in power respond accordingly. For example, Barbara Crossette reports in the *New York Times* (7 April 1991) about an incident in Batamaloo, Kashmir:

> In this conservative Muslim society, women have moved to the forefront of demonstrations and also into guerilla conclaves. No single event has contributed more to this rapidly rising militancy among women than reports of a gang rape a month ago by Indian troops in Kunan, a remote village in northwestern Kashmir.
>
> According to a report filed by S. M. Yasin, district magistrate in Kupwara, the regional center, the armed forces "behaved like violent beasts." He identified them as members of the Fourth Rajputana Rifles and said that they rampage through the village from 11 P.M. on Feb. 23 until 9 the next morning.
>
> "A large number of armed personnel entered into the houses of villagers and at gunpoint they gang-raped 23 ladies, without any consideration of their age, married, unmarried,

pregnancy etc.," he wrote. "There was a hue and cry in the whole village." Local people say that as many as 100 women were molested in some way.

As a man of African descent, I would like to think that Africans have some special insight, enlightened hearts, or love in us that calms us in such times of madness. My romanticism is shattered every day as I observe Black communities across this land. The number of rapes reported and unreported in our communities is only the latest and most painful example of how far we have drifted from beauty. However, it is seldom that I have hurt more than when I learned about the "night of terror" that occurred in Meru, Kenya, on July 13, 1991, at the St. Kizito Boarding School. A high school protest initiated by the boys, in which the girls refused to join, resulted in a night of death, rapes, and beatings unparalleled in modern Kenya, in Africa, or the world. As Timothy Dwyer reported in the *Chicago Tribune* (18 August 1991):

> The night of terror a month ago at the boarding school near Mount Kenya has torn the soul of the Kenyan people. What had the girls done to invoke the wrath of their male school-mates? They dared say no to the boys, who wanted them to join a protest against the school's headmaster, according to police and to those girls who lived through the night.
>
> In Kenya, one-party rule has resulted in a tyranny of the majority. Dissent, even in politics, is not welcome. "Here, the minority must always go along with the majority's wishes," said a businessman who has done a lot of work with the government in the last 15 years and asked not to be named. "And it is said that a woman cannot say no to a man."
>
> Woman's groups have said the rapes and deaths were an extreme metaphor for what goes on in the Kenyan society. The girls of St. Kizito dared to say no to the boys, and 19 paid with their lives while 71 others were beaten and raped...
>
> There have been many school protests in Kenya this year. This summer alone, some 20 protests have turned into riots

resulting in the destruction of school property. There have
been rapes at other schools when girls have refused to join
boys in their protests.

A growing part of the answer is that we men, as difficult
as it may seem, must view all women (no matter who they
are—race, culture, religion, or nationality) as extended family.
The question is, and I know that I am stretching, would we rape
our mothers, grandmothers, sisters, or other female relatives, or
even give such acts a first thought? Can we extend this attitude
to all women? Therefore, we must:

1. Teach our sons that it is their responsibility to be anti-
    rapist; they must be counter-rapist in thought, conversa-
    tions, raps, organizations, and actions.

2. Teach our daughters how to defend themselves and main-
    tain an uncompromising stance toward men and boys.

3. Understand that being a counter-rapist is honorable, manly,
    and necessary for a just society.

4. Understand that anti-rapist actions are part of the Black
    tradition; being an anti-rapist is in keeping with the best of
    African culture, family and extended family configura-
    tions. Even in times of war, we were known to honor and
    respect the personhood of children and women.

5. Be glowing examples of men who are fighting to treat
    women as equals. Be fair and just in our associations with
    women. This means at the core that families as now
    defined and constructed must continually be re-assessed.
    In today's economy most women, married and unmarried,
    must work. We men must encourage women in their work
    and must be intimately involved with housework and the

rearing of children.

6.   Try to understand that just as men are different from one another, women also differ; therefore we must try not to stereotype women into the limiting and often debilitating expectations of men. We must encourage and support them in their searching and development.

7.   Be unafraid of independent, intelligent and self-reliant women. And by extension, understand that intelligent women think for themselves and may not want to have sex with a particular man. This is a woman's prerogative and is not a comment on anything else other than the fact that she does not want to have sex.

8.   Be bold and strong enough to stop other men (relatives, friends, or strangers) from raping and to intervene in a rape in process with the fury and destruction of a hurricane against the rapist.

9.   Listen to women. Listen to women, especially to womanist/feminist/Pan-Africanist philosophies of life. Also, study the writings of women, especially Black women.

10.   Act responsibly to the listening and studying. Be a part of and support anti-rape groups for boys and men. Introduce anti-rape discussion into men's groups and organizations.

11.   Never stop growing. Understand that growth is limited and limiting without the input of intelligent women.

12.   Learn to love. Study love. Even if one is at war, if there is to be a sane and livable world, love and respect, respect and love must conquer. Rape is anti-love, anti-respect. Love is not easy. One does not fall in love but *grows* into love.

We can put to rest the rape problem in one generation if its eradication is as important to us as our cars, jobs, careers, sport-games, beer, and quest for power. However, the women who put rape on the front burners must continue to challenge us and their own cultural training, and position themselves so that they and their messages are not compromised or ignored.

A significant few of their
fathers, brothers, husbands, sons
and growing strangers
are willing to unleash harm onto the earth
and spill blood in the eyes
of
maggots in running shoes
who do not know the sounds of birth
or respect the privacy of the human form

If we are to be just in our internal rebuilding, we must challenge tradition and cultural ways of life that relegate women to inferior status in the home, church/mosque/temple, workplace, political life, and education. Men are not born rapists; we are taught very subtly, often in unspoken ways, that women are ours for the taking. Generally, such teachings begin in the family. Enlightenment demands fairness, impartiality and vision; it demands confrontation of outdated definitions and acceptance of fair and just resolutions. One's sex, race, social class, or wealth should not determine entitlements or justice. If we are honest, men must be in the forefront of eradicating sex stereotypes in all facets of private and public life. Being honest, as difficult and as self-incriminating as it may be, is the only way that we can truly liberate ourselves. If men can liberate themselves (with the help of women) from the negative aspects of the culture that produced them, maybe a just, fair, good, and liberated society is possible in our lifetime.

The liberation of the male psyche from one of domination, power, hunger, control, and absolute rightness requires an honest and fair assessment of patriarchal culture. This requires commitment to deep study, combined with a willingness to undergo painful, uncomfortable, and often shocking change. We are not where we should be. That is why rape exists; why families are so easily formed and just as easily dissolved; why children are confused and abused; why our elderly are discarded, abused and exploited; and why teenage boys create substitute families (gangs) that terrorize their own communities.

I remain an optimistic realist primarily because I love life and most of what it has to offer. I often look at my children and tears come to my eyes because I realize how blessed I am to be their father. My wife and the other women in my life are special because they know that they are special and have taken it upon themselves, at great cost, to actualize their dreams, making what was considered unthinkable for many of them a few years ago a reality today. If we men, of all races, cultures, and continents would just examine the inequalities of power that exist in our "own" families, businesses, political and spiritual institutions, and decide today to reassess and re-configure them in consultations with the women in our lives, we would succeed in doing the most fundamental corrective act of a counter-rapist.

It is indeed significant, and not an arbitrary side-note, that males and females are created biologically different. These profound differences are partially why we are attracted to each other and are also what is beautiful about life. But too often, due to hierarchy and patriarchal definitions, one's gender also relegates one to a "position" in life that is not necessarily respected. Gender should not determine moral or economic worth, as it now does in too many cultures. In a just society, one's knowledge and capabilities—what one is actually able to contribute to the world—is more valuable than if the person is male or female.

Respect for the women closest to us can give us the strength and knowledge to confront the "animal" in us with regard to the women we consider "others." Also, keep in mind that the "others" often are the women closest to us. If we honestly confront the traditions and histories that have shaped us, we may come to the realization that women should be encouraged to go as far as their intellect and talents will take them—burdened only by the obstacles that affect all of us. Most certainly the sexual energies of men must be checked before our misguided maleness manifests itself in the most horrible of crimes—rape.

No!
means No!
even when men think
that they are "god's gift to women"
even after dropping a week's check & more
on dinner by the ocean,
the four tops, temptations and intruders memory tour,
imported wine & roses that captured her smile,
suggesting to you private music & low lights
drowning out her unarticulated doubts.

Question the thousand years teachings
crawling through your lower depths   and
don't let your little head
out think your big head.

No! means No!
even when her signals suggest yes.

ULTIMATE CONFUSION

Women, Men and Self Hatred

One of the great tragedies of modern education is that most people are not taught to think critically. That is, the majority of the world's people, the West included, are taught to *believe* rather than *think*. Seldom do most people think seriously about that which they are taught to believe because we are all creatures of imitation and habit. If something was good enough for our parents, we generally accept it as good enough for us—whether *it* is religion, history, politics, sex-roles, or television sitcoms.

Ignorance is visited upon the African American community daily in the form of smiling politicians, culturally insensitive merchants, greedy landlords, teachers with baby-setter mentalities, and rappin' young brothers working in the "underground" economy who have absolutely no understanding of their importance to the Black community. It is not unusual for ignorant people to talk about how ignorant other people are. We are taught to memorize uninteresting and often unimportant "facts" and "theories" rather than given insight into how to cope with and solve the difficult personal and public obstacles confronting us. As a result of this grim situation, most people's thinking does not lead to long-term solutions. More often than not, especially for the poor, this lack of critical thinking leads to the creation of more problems. Therefore, if one does not have the "correct" education to attack and eradicate problems emanating from this racist, service-oriented, information-gathering, corporate economy, and technologically oppressive society, all one is left with is one's own "practical" experience and "home-based" knowledge to work with.

Often, this "home-based" education only equips one to survive in one's limited community (plantation) at a subsistence level. African Americans who do not have access to the latest information or functional knowledge needed to understand and participate in a market economy are generally rendered powerless in their own communities and are insignificant at city, state, national or international levels. Such a condition of powerlessness stems from not comprehending current racial, political, and economic realities. It is also the product of accepting incorrect or bad ideas. Most Black people have been swimming between bad, marginal, and worthless information since our forced migration to this land.

Ideas as Weapons

Ideas and their creators run the world. Christianity is an idea. Islam is an idea. Buddhism and Hinduism are ideas. Politics, science, and technology are the results of ideas. Capitalism and Socialism were ideas before they became reality. Mathematics and physics grew from the imaginations of creative people. One's place in the world is partly due to the ideas that a culture has forced on one, and/or the ideas that a person "freely" accepts and uses. Concepts of manhood and womanhood are genetically/biologically mandated as well as the results of acculturation. Most cultures in the world are dominated by the male imperative. That is, most nation-states revolve around and are fueled by the ideas of men. This speaks in part to why the world is in such a wretched state.

Men and women are socialized and nurtured differently. Generally, men are taught (educated) to run the world, or run "things" in the world. Women, on the downside, are taught (trained) to work and do the bidding of men in the world. There are women who run things; however, they are in the acute minority, and the things that they are in charge of are not defined as critical or important to the state's existence. Most people, men and women, as a result of universal patriarchal culture, believe without question that this is *normal* and therefore *right*. Why? Because "we have always done it this way."

One of the latest contributions to such sexist nonsense is Shahrazad Ali's *The Blackman's Guide to Understanding the Blackwoman*. This is a 189-page manual that contributes greatly to the misunderstanding of African American women. Ms. Ali has written and self-published a document that not only diminishes the intelligence and motives of Black women, but, in the final analysis, misrepresents them as foul-mouthed, evil-thinking pea-heads whose only goal in life is to "get over" on Black men.

She does not gather *facts* to document such assertions; instead, what she gives us is gossip, hearsay, family history, and "women's magazine psychology." What I find most upsetting about this book is its misinformation and gross generalizations masquerading as "facts" and "secrets" and the willingness of a significant number of Black people, mainly Black men, to accept her "kitchen" and "beauty shop" talk as God-given truth. This semi-autobiographical work is rank opportunism. However, because of its subject matter, it has attracted the attention of a great number of naive men who have been looking for such a document to validates their male chauvinist views of Black women.

Ms. Ali's book is a self-hating, victim's report on a very limited Black woman community that she generalizes to the entire Black woman population. Yes, I'm sure there are *some* African American women who are described accurately here. But, to claim that this book offers a representative portrait of half of the African American population is to do an injustice to the language and reduce the lives of Black women to the level of a negro soap opera played in white-face.

Worldview

Black women the world over have been the steel holding the Black world together. Black women have had to engage in any and all the work that was/is available to keep the family and "nation" alive. In the 1990s Black women do more than their share of life-giving and life-saving work. Most of this work is not intellectually taxing. For example, in Africa, women do seventy-five percent of the agricultural work and ninety-five percent of the domestic work; in Mozambique, ninety percent of the women are engaged in food production; African women do seventy percent of the hoeing and weeding, sixty percent of harvesting, fifty percent of the planting, sixty percent of the marketing, ninety percent of the food processing, and eighty percent of the work involved in transporting crops home and storing them (*New Internationalist*, June 1990). The men are involved in the mismanagement of African states and the grafting of eleven or more wars being waged in Africa today.

African American women do not have the "best" jobs in this country. In terms of the Black community, they do whatever they can to put food on the table, clothe and educate their children, help pay rent or mortgages, and make the *many* necessary sacrifices that aid a great number of our children to escape America's deadly traps. Most of these women are *without male partners* (sixty-two percent) and must depend on their own ingenuity and extended family for development. This is not to suggest that millions of conscious and caring Black men are not contributing significantly also, but due to the nature of our struggle, it is clear that Black women are doing *more* than their share—especially in terms of child-rearing. To state otherwise displays abominable ignorance of this culture and its debilitating systems of white supremacy.

Bogus Arguments

Ms. Ali's arguments reduce history to the conversations she has had with herself, friends, and her extended family. *The Blackman's Guide* is a pseudo-Islamic-Black-Muslim-Nationalist position stating where she believes Black women should be. If this book had been written by a Black man, white man, or white woman, he or she would not be able to show his or her face in the Black community without serious confrontation. The *only* reason this slander is being received with any currency in the African American community is because the author is Black, female, Muslim and/or nationalist, and its title is a good example of how, with the right packaging, anything will sell. The following is a representative sample of what the unsuspecting public is buying in *The Blackman's Guide*.

On sex:

> Since she is such a pseudo romantic creature she cannot be trusted in the presence of strange men for a long length of time because she is always open for a line, especially if it's one telling her how beautiful or desirable she is. She

believes anything a Blackman tells her as long as he looks
good to her physically (146).

She brags on her sexual conquests in the same way the
Blackman is rumored to brag about his. She will explain to
her friends in great detail about her activities in bed with a
Blackman. She especially likes to tell about the size of his
penis, what he says while copulating, his stroke, and whether
or not he performed oral sex well. They go into minute by
minute, blow by blow description about the encounter. If he
does any oddities she calls him nasty and other horrible
names and she and her friends laugh at him. It is a rare
Blackwoman who does not tell about her private sexual life
with a Blackman. So if a Blackman has a woman with a best
friend or several close friends he can be sure that they know
all about his bedroom action. Down to the most intimate
detail (147).

On confidentiality and trust:

The Blackman has allowed himself to be devalued by
Blackwomen who rank among the most confused species of
humanhood on the planet Earth... (46).

Blackwomen reveal all of the Blackmen's personal business
to her friends. If the Blackman has any special information
he tells his woman in confidence you can be sure that her best
friend or her family members know too. She takes a special
glee in letting her friends know the most intimate details and
secrets—even his antics in bed, and anything else of personal and confidential nature. She does not consider that a
confidence has been violated, nor that it is unfair to the
Blackman who entrusted her with the information. NO
Blackwoman ever tells another Blackwoman that she is
wrong to tell her man's business to the public. This process
is an agreed and acceptable dialogue among Blackwomen. It
is also certain that some of the information she tells her
girlfriends ends up being whispered into the ears of her
girlfriend's man. The Blackman is betrayed twice this way.
His business is all over town and he doesn't even know it.
She tells everything. Everything. No subject is too private
or too sacred (47-48).

On social integration:

The Blackwoman will date, and as reported daily, will marry
a whiteman. She finds her relationship with the whiteman

perhaps the answer to all her dreams and fantasies. First, he is removed for the Black experience, and brings a new set of rules to the involvement. Second, he represents the culmination of every movie and T.V. show she has ever seen featuring a gallant white beau who knows how to treat a woman and swoops in always coming to her rescue. Third, he is an alternative set of men whom she believes can be utilized because of the nonavailability of Blackmen. Now that there appears to be fewer Blackmen, and she can't get along with any of them, she is pursuing other races to see what she can see (53).

On arguments:

This brings up a very unpopular and unpleasant category—the Blackman's self-defense mechanism. There is never an excuse for ever hitting a Blackwoman anywhere but in the mouth. Because it is from that hole, in the lower part of her face, that all her rebellion culminates into words. Her unbridled tongue is a main reason she cannot get along with the Blackman. She often needs a reminder. This does not mean that she needs, or wants, to be battered or beaten to a bloody pulp. However, if she ignores that authority and superiority of the Blackman, there is a penalty. When she crosses this line and becomes viciously insulting it is time for the Blackman to soundly slap her in the mouth. She is often like a rambunctious child. She wants to know what her parameters are. If she is allowed to curse at and yell at the Blackman she will get worse (169).

Conclusion:

Every chapter in this book is filled with examples of the problems the Blackwoman has both emotionally and mentally. Until the Blackman is able to collectively access the amount of psychological damage done to the character of the Blackwoman he cannot know where of how to begin correcting it. It's deep. It's an infection that for any years has robbed the Blackman from reaching his full potential as the king of kings. He is held back by his queen who is deeply entrenched in fear. Fear that she will be recognized and required to change. She is trying to run away from the problem. She is trying to flee from the individual work that must be done to save our nation. Although not lazy by nature, she has become loose and careless, about herself, and about her man and her family. Her brain is smaller than the

Blackman's so while she is acclaimed for her high scholastic achievement, her thought processes do not compare to the conscious Blackman's. Her complaints and whining about the lack of qualified Blackmen has led her to whitemen, celibacy and lesbianism. She would rather live in the artificial stages of these type of random poorly thought out choices than accept the options offered to her by the Blackman. As the first, the original, and the leader, the Blackman is responsible for making the Blackwoman into what she must become (177).

Need I comment on the above statements? These are five out of hundreds of ignorant and demeaning assertions that go unsubstantiated. How can intelligent Black men buy into this nonsense, unless Black men want to believe the worst about Black women anyway? However, to really understand how vicious and dangerous this dribble is, let us re-write the first two quotes changing all feminine designations to masculine:

Since he is such a pseudo romantic creature he cannot be trusted in the presence of strange women for a long length of time because he is always open for a line, especially if it's one telling him how handsome or desirable he is. He believes anything a Blackwoman tells him if she looks good to him physically.

He brags on his sexual conquests in the same way the Blackwoman is rumored to brag about hers. He will explain to his friends in great detail about his activities in bed with a Blackwoman. He especially likes to tell about the size of her vagina, what she says while copulating, her stroke, and whether or not she performed oral sex well. They go into minute by minute, blow by blow description about the encounter. If she does any oddities he calls her nasty and other horrible names and he and his friends laugh at her. It is a rare Blackman who

does not tell about his private sexual life with a Blackwoman.
So if a Blackwoman has a man with a best friend or several
close friends she can be sure that they know all about her
bedroom action. Down to the most intimate detail.

Honestly, would not most Black men be horrified to read
such gutter insanity about themselves? At best, this book is an
opportunistic diatribe against Black women that patronizes
Black men. It purports to aid Black men by giving us insights
into Black womanhood. For the uninformed Black man, this
book is a never-ending guide to nonfunctional relationships. It
is a call to return to the non-questioning patriarch, the return of
the mythic Black king. I suppose he is to rule over a mindless
family and apartment. This book is a call to put and keep Black
women in their "place" as defined by Black men. Sounds like
a return to slavery to me, with Black men replacing the white
slave traders.

Conclusions

The last time I was this upset about a piece of work was when
I saw Melvin Van Peebles' movie *Sweet, Sweet Badass Song*. I
gave it a negative review in *Black World* magazine. Ms. Ali has
published a petty piece of propaganda that duplicates the racist
materials that we have been fighting against for the last 400 years.
Ms. Ali feels safe attacking and demeaning other Black women
primarily because she does not respect or identify with them. She
is really an "outsider" using the hurt, pain, insecurities, fragile
egos, and negative self-concepts of Black women as the foundation for this rather enlightened look at herself.

The cultural memory of a people is stored in its literature.
There are too many unthinking Black people who will use *The*

Blackman's Guide as a rationale for their medieval actions toward each other. What will our children and grandchildren think of us if this pure garbage goes unchallenged? I write this response for my daughters and sons. The future of Black people lies in the loveships and partnerships that Black women and men form and build upon.

As I complete this essay, I am reminded of the time I took my son to a young scientist summer program at one of the local universities. He was twelve years old. About half of the young people there were girls between the ages of ten and fifteen. The program introduces them to the fields of science, engineering and architecture. What are we to tell these young girls? Stop studying in the traditional male domains? Research housework, closet-cleaning and child-rearing only. Follow Black men uncritically wherever the wind blows and do it with a smile, preferably pregnant. Are we to deny Black girls a chance to learn the critical skills needed to change the course of the world for the better? I say no! This world prepares daily for the failure and death of our people. I cannot in good conscience take part in restricting the intellectual development of my daughters or other Black females. The real reason for *The Blackman's Guide* can be found in the author's need for fame, recognition, money, and justification for her own lifestyle. The essence of Black manhood cannot be found in oppressing Black women or anyone else.

PRISONS

Rage and Young Black Male Destruction*

The 1971 uprising at Attica Correctional Facility placed the prison movement for reform and prisoners' rights on the front pages of newspapers across the nation. Attica, after twenty years, is still being argued in the courts. Few who followed the Black-led rebellion can forget the hurricane of state troopers and guards on September 13, rushing like dogs in heat to retake the prison under the muted shouts of "save me a nigger." Malcolm Bell's *The Turkey Shoot* documents that horrible episode and its attempted cover-up.[1] Attica is the perfect metaphor for 200 years of prison misdevelopment in the United States: prisons don't work.

According to Lee H. Bowker's *Prison Victimization*, the prison system in the United States is modern slavery, and those who suffer the greatest are African Americans and other people of color.[2] It is now common knowledge that in the American criminal justice system, money talks and everybody else does time. The major people involved in criminal activity in

---

* Forward to *A Call to Action*, ed. by Linda Thurston, the 1991 American Friends Service Committee's National Commission on Crime and Justice.

1. Bell M., The Turkey Shoot: Tracking the Attica Cover-up (New York: Grover Press), 1985.
2. Bowker, L.H., Prison Victimization (New York: Elfevevier Publishers), 1980.

America are not people of color but white men. Yet a survey of prison and jail inhabitants will reveal that these institutions have become the final answer for the victims of poverty, the mentally and culturally different, inadequately educated, un-employed, and non-white.

According to the National Institute of Justice, in states with large inner-city populations, the percentage of incarcer-ated persons who are African American is 83 percent. The one-in-four figure of Black males involved in the criminal justice system, documented by the Sentencing Project of Washington, DC, will surely double for the group aged 18 to 29 if current trends continue.[3] This does not even include the 66 percent of women behind bars who are African American.

That over 60 percent of the prison population is poor and of color only confirms for the thinking person that if one wishes to indulge in serious crime in America, it is best to earn an MBA or law degree. The Savings and Loans bandits and their kind do not go to Attica-like facilities but to "country clubs with fences and tennis courts"—if they are incarcerated at all. It is common political wisdom that anything goes in America as long as one does not get caught. From Panama to Iraq to the cities of the heartland, America's capacity to destroy lives has been documented. Yet the call from overzealous politicians is to build bigger prisons, more prisons, and harsher prisons—not for the multi-million dollar criminals of America, but for the dispossessed.

The call for increased imprisonment is in keeping with the short-sighted economic development projected for states from

---

3. Mauer, M., "Young Black Men and the Criminal Justice System: A Growing National Problem," The Sentencing Project (February 1990).

Michigan to California, where prison building and staffing is big business. In the federal anti-crime package of 1989, President Bush proposed spending $1.2 billion—with $1 billion for the construction of new federal prisons to house 24,000 additional prisoners. Private enterprise also has gotten into the act. The WRI Group of Shreveport, Louisiana, has proposed to build prisons in East Texas for the sole purpose of importing prisoners from over-crowded areas like the District of Columbia, California and New York State.[4]

Currently, the criminal justice system is a $35 billion industry. Future profits from privatization of prisons could be enormous. With states paying anywhere from $28 to $65 per day per prisoner, investors could recoup their money in less than ten years and turn the prisons over to the states after twenty years with ten years of clear profits. This type of arrangement will allow investors to earn substantial returns on their investment, profits that will likely go untaxed because of special arrangements with local municipalities.

Local politicians are listening to these ideas as an alternative to passing bond proposals and building prisons with tax dollars. The projects are especially popular in states with large urban populations where existing prisons are already over-crowded and arrests and convictions of persons of color are continuing at a break-neck pace. For example, in Louisiana there are 15,000 outstanding warrants; in California, over 30,000 outstanding warrants; and in the city of Chicago, approximately 25,000.[5]

---

4. Robert, R. E., Program Director, Inmate Community Program, Sidell, Louisiana, conversation with Haki Madhubuti.
5. Ibid.

To understand prisons in American society, it is not only necessary to make distinctions between right and wrong, good and evil, lawful and unlawful; we must also look at poverty and fear, politics and economy, and race and racism. It is clear that the roots of crime lie deep in the social structure and culture of this country. The current attitude toward incarceration is a "lock them up and bury the key" mentality. This attitude is like a cancer in the blood, and, like polluted water, is deadly to us all. For many of those in prisons, a connection to family and community is missing in their lives, while an allegiance to America's negative values is present. For African Americans, Latinos, Asian Americans, Native Americans, and others, life in the United States is like walking barefoot on razor-sharp rolled wire. Prisons cannot heal those wounds. In fact, the mistreatment of prisoners while incarcerated does not lead to rehabilitation, but, rather, to a greater propensity for criminal activity for many.

Certainly the cost of ignorance is high, and as a nation we will continue to go deeper into debt as long as all we do is talk about the problems and lock people up. That is why this our efforts must be more than just talk. We must work toward mobilization and change. Certainly we will have failed in our mission if our efforts only soothe the consciences of a few. Until and unless we address the social problems of America, crime will rage unabated in our streets. A dysfunctional culture produces dysfunctional people. The solutions to our problems of crime lie not in prisons but in providing for all people a way to productively live their lives.

Missing Movements, Missing Fathers

Black Male Responsibility in the Lives of Children

I entered adulthood in the 1960s right out of the U.S. Army into the streets of Chicago to be absorbed by the Black Arts, Civil Rights, and Black Power movements. These movements saved my life and gave greater meaning and cultural* purpose to me, a young Black man fresh out of the military. Most of my life, I had been subtly taught to hate myself and my people. For the three years of military service, I had also been taught to kill people who looked like me.

These movements, which encompassed all of the 1960s and part of the 1970s, cannot be dismissed by draft-dodging vice presidents and self-righteous politicians born with privilege in their oatmeal. Scores of contemporary revisionist historians and political scientists are now trying to paint the movements of the 1960s as destructive forces in American life. This may indeed be a serious consideration from their point of view. However, most participants in these movements felt that the struggle to share local, state, and federal power; the opening up of public facilities to all on an equal basis; the empowering

---

* I am using the word "culture" to denote a working system of values, attitudes, and institutions (from the family to the U.S. government) that influences individual and group behavior in all areas of human activity: law, education, arts, politics, agriculture, language, the military, sports, entertainment, health, economics, and social development.

of the disenfranchised with the vote; the recapturing and redefining of the Black/African image in the American/world mind; the equal participation in the educational process by the underserved; the enlargement of living and work space for people of color; the redefinition of what it means to be a woman in a male-dominant society; and the open and raw disclosures of the worldwide destructive powers of racism (white world supremacy) in maintaining a Nazi-like world from South Africa to South Carolina is what the Black movement of the 1960s and early 1970s was about.

The Rodney King incident, as well as the pre- and post-beating verdict, only helps to sharpen our focus on the political reality of young Black men in today's America. Obviously, one's perspective is always open to question. The difference between knowing and not knowing in a cultural/political context such as the United States is a larger question than just the quality of one's formal education. This is why the Black movement was so important and instrumental in the political/cultural development of millions of people; it gave us a context to find and investigate content. If nothing else, we learned the right questions to ask. The battle lines were not always clear. It was not always white vs. Black, white Christians vs. Black Christians vs. Black Muslims vs. Jews, Black politicians vs. Black activists, negro vs. Black vs. African, capitalists vs. socialists vs. communists —and we can go on and on. The complexity of Black struggle has always been at the heart of our reactions. W. E. B. Du Bois's groundbreaking *The Souls of Black Folk,* Harold Cruse's *The Crisis of the Negro Intellectual* and Frances Cress Welsing's *The Isis Papers: the Keys to the Colors* all delineate the difficulty involved in deciding "a way" to move a people from "enslavement" to liberation.

However, the major point is that the Black movement provided young African Americans of that period a context for discovering identity and purpose, and it also provided them serious proposals for the future. The movement prevented many young women and men from being swallowed by the ever-present lowest common denominator: street culture. This movement existed as extended family, developing a culture that was productive and caring. Involvement in the movement provided young people with something to care about that was not insulting to their own personhood. It defined relationships and challenged us to defend our own limited resources. But one of the major contributions was in the arena of ideas.

For the first time in the lives of many of us, we were confronted with ethical, moral, spiritual, political, historical, and economic questions and dilemmas. Through our day-to-day activities, we were forced to think at another level about the United States and the world. Often our lives depended upon the quality of our thinking and decisions. Such critical thinking at such a young age matured many of us, and we began to see our struggle as one deeply attached to international realities and liberation struggles in other parts of the world. We were reading, on our own, the works of Carter G. Woodson, Frantz Fanon, Amical Cabral, E. Franklin Frazier, Gwendolyn Brooks, Margaret Walker, Richard Wright, John O. Killens, Kwame Nkrumah, Julius Nyerere, Marcus Garvey and others.

The Black movement does not exist today as it did in the 1960s. This is not to suggest that there are no movements today. The profound difference, however, is that no national Black political movement exists of any consequence. Even during the 1960s and 1970s there were many streams, but there was only one river. There existed a national consensus on broadly defined goals and objectives. Whether one worked in the NAACP, CORE, SNCC, SCLC, the Urban League, NOI, Black Panther Party, US Organization, CAP* or the Black Arts and Southern Student Movements, one had a connection, a force, a greater purpose and definition than one's personal geography.

The political and cultural realities of today are just as oppressive as the past, but the vehicle to combat them does not exist at a national level. We are fighting the same battles, but our national movement has been torn asunder, and most of our young are not being nurtured into struggle at a responsible level. Many young people who are industrious do find local community-based organizations and socially committed churches in which to work. However, the great majority of youth find themselves seeking answers in the streets.

During the 1960s, whether our national spokesperson was Martin Luther King, Malcolm X, Stokely Carmichael (now Kwame Toure) or Angela Davis, there was a feeling of "going together" and of watching each others' backs. It did not matter too much if one wore African dress, a suit and bow tie, or overalls, the movement kept many of us busy and working for a higher goal. This movement minimized gang, drug and criminal activity in our communities. That such a movement does not exist today speaks loudly to our failure as a people to develop a *leadership* that understands the force and power of

---

* National Association for the Advancement of Colored People, Congress on Racial Equality, Student Nonviolent Coordinating Committee, Southern Christian Leadership Conference, Nation of Islam, Congress of African People.

national organizations that function around the power of ideas rather than egos. This leadership has not developed replacements that it can support and guide. This short-sightedness has left most young men and women with no alternative for survival than going to the streets.

Street culture is a culture of containment, and most young people do not realize that it all too often leads to a dead end. Street culture, as I am using the term, is a counter-force to movement culture. Street culture in today's urban reality denotes survival at all cost. This worldview is mostly negative because it demands constant adjusting to circumstances that are often beyond young people's control or understanding such as economics, education, housing, jobs, food, law, etc. In urban America, traveling to and from school, church, work, welfare offices or recreation can be and often are life and death choices for young people, mainly young males. There is no national or local political/cultural Black movement to direct or protect our youth today.

Fathers and Family

If culturally focused/politically clear and responsible Black fathers/parents were a majority in the African-American family and community, there would not be a gang, drug or crime problem at the level that exists today. This is not to suggest that gangs, drugs, or crime would not exist in our communities, but these elements would not rule or run our communities as they now do in too many instances. Fathers as parents in working families do make a difference. Black women single-parents, against great odds, are fighting a losing battle, and responsible and dependable fathers, grandfathers, uncles, and other men of our extended family are critically needed.

One need not repeat the statistics detailing the decline of Black children born into two-parent households. The figures do not speak well of the Black community. Marriage, whether "legal" (sanctioned by the courts), or common-law (people deciding to live together without legal documents), is on the decline. However, the babies do not stop coming, and the music and love so badly needed in the rearing of children are disappearing quickly from the African-American community.

Stable families and communities are absolutely necessary if we are to have productive and loving individuals. Marriage represents the foundation of family. Without marriage (a bonding tradition that sanctions and forces "partners" into commitments beyond the bedroom), families soon dissolve; or other types of families form. Families are the foundation for community. Like a family, a functional community provides security, caring, wealth, resources, cultural institutions, education, employment, a spiritual force, shelter, and a challenging atmosphere. Families and community shape the individual into either a productive or non-productive person. Without family, without community, individuals are left to an "everything is everything" existence. And if "everything is everything," "nothing is nothing."

Fathers/parents are the missing links in the lives of many young African Americans. In an increasingly dangerous and unpredictable world, the absence of fathers adds tremendously to the insecurity of children. It is common knowledge that children function best in an atmosphere where both parents combine and complement their energies and talents in the rearing of children. Even if pregnancy is an accident, it is clear that once a decision is made to bring a child to term, the rearing of that child cannot be accidental. Most children are born at the top of their game, genius level. It is the socialization process that turns most creative, talented, and normal children into dependent and helpless adults.

In a patriarchal society, Black men must be able to offer their families a measure of protection and, at a minimum, basic life-giving needs, such as clothing, shelter, food, education, and security. The West and most of the world define manhood as the ability to protect and provide for one's family. If a man does not do that, according to most cultures, he is incomplete (i.e., not a man). A good many Black men are not able to deliver in these two areas. Some of the reasons for this include:

1. White world supremacy (racism)—Black men are one of the major threats to white male rule.
2. Failure of integration—Many Black men believe(d) America's big lie of the melting pot theory.
3. Failure of national and local welfare systems—the development of a beggar's mentality among many Black people.
4. Failure of public education.
5. Changing economic system—increased dependency on the state. The destruction of Black families and family values.
6. Replacement of Black men in the market place with white women and teenagers.
7. Loss of self-respect, self-esteem, and self-love.
8. Ignorance of our own history and accomplishments.
9. Unawareness of changing world realities.
10. Lack of skills—especially business skills.
11. Fear.
12. Not understanding power and power relationships.

For conscious men, none of this should be new. However, in this war situation that we live in, the circumstances demand that Black men rise to the challenge. And a great part of that challenge is to be responsible husbands, fathers, and parents. Without all of these, a bright future is doubtful. Being a good and fruitful husband, father, and parent may be the most difficult task facing African American men.

We now live in a time, a first in our history, when there are millions of African-American children with absent fathers. Other than the period of chattel slavery, there has never been a time when the absence of Black fathers has been so grim. This tide of absent, unavailable, nonfunctioning fathers must be reversed. There are no easy solutions.

Fathering for most Black men is learned on the job. Generally, by that time, for many fathers it is too late. There are few classes in fathering. Fathering is a learned process. Most Black men give very little thought to the lifelong commitment that fathers must make to their children.

Children learn to do most things by watching and imitating their parents or care-givers. Formal education starts generally at the age of five for most children and at two-and-a-half for the blessed few who are able to benefit from Headstart or private schools. Children learn to be mothers or fathers by observing and studying their mothers, fathers, grandparents, aunts, uncles, and television.

These days most Black boys learn to be fathers by watching the wind (the spaces reserved for missing fathers). Many of them also receive instruction in fathering from their mothers' discussions about absent "dads" or whatever names these men are given. If anything is clear about the African-American community today, it is that Black women are having serious difficulty teaching Black boys to be men and, by extension, to be fathers.

However, this is not a condemnation of Black women/ mothers who are trying, against great odds, to raise their sons into responsible and recognizable Black men.   The facts suggest that many of them are not succeeding, and the facts also suggest that it is ignorant, stupid, and insensitive to blame Black women for not raising strong Black men.   The music in these women's lives is little.   To be left alone to raise the children may be an impossible task for many of them.   Yet we do know that millions of African American women rise to the challenge and are responsible for millions of Black men who have made "successful" transitions from boyhood to manhood.

Again, it is not easy. There is a difference between raising children and rearing them.   Mari Evans, in a very important essay, "The Relationship of Child-Rearing Practices to Chaos and Change in the African American Family," states:

> ...raising [children] is "providing for," while rearing is "responding to." Raising can be satisfied by providing the essentials: food, shelter, clothing and reasonable care. "Rearing" is a carefully thought out process. Rearing begins with a goal and is supported by a clear view of what are facts and what is truth (and the two are not necessarily synonymous).   Rearing is complex and requires sacrifice and dedication.   It is an ongoing process of "preparation." Joe Kennedy reared presidents; the British royal family rears heirs to the English throne; and when a young African doctor, born in the continent and presently in self-exile in a neighboring country because of her ANC (African National Congress) commitment was interviewed on the news recently and was asked if she was not afraid for her four-year-old son, given her political activism, said, "He has a duty to lay down his life for his people," she announced the rearing of a "race man"....Obviously something different, some

> carefully thought out process, some long-range political
> view is present when one has a clear sense of one's own
> reality and therefore intends to rear presidents, rulers, or free
> men and women.

Mari Evans, in her own unique and poetic manner, has set forth the challenge for African American people, the rearing of "race men and women."

If fathers give some thought to this, they will understand that fathering (parenting) is also a political act. As a colonized people fighting for survival and development, African Americans must see our children as future "warriors" in this struggle for liberation. Mari Evans defined colonization as "suppression and exploitation designed to keep a people powerless, dependent, subordinate, and mystified." We are at war for the minds, bodies, souls, spirits and futures of our children. Ms. Evans states it this way:

> Child-rearing should be the primary concern of an oppressed
> people, and although the rearing of race men and women is
> obviously a stressful, complex and tedious process, it should
> be entered into at birth.

We Black men cannot depend on others to do our job. Fathering must be as important to us as love-making (sex). It is easy to make babies, but difficult to rear them. We have to embrace and highlight the culture of family and familial responsibility. If men continue to have sex, babies will come and our contribution to our children's development must be maximized and of a quality nature.

Some Considerations

Many men will have to confront the definitions of fatherhood that they received from their own fathers and the rest of society at large. I am sure that there is conflict here for most men. In my own case, it is now easy for me to state quite clearly that I do not know my father. To be honest, all that I can say of him is that as a child I feared him. When around him, I did not hear much more than criticism of one form or another. He was not there for me or my sister when we needed him most. Now, in the middle of my years, I have accepted his noninvolvement in my development as a lesson not to be repeated with my own children.

However, I do not perceive the distance, noninvolvement and lack of financial support from my father toward me as a source of hatred or negative feeling toward him. As a man and as a father/parent, I now realize that his choices were determined as a result of the condition under which he lived and the knowledge that influenced his decisions. That I was not a priority on his list hurt, but how long does one carry such hurt? How long does one allow such hurt to stop one from developing into the man, father, and parent that one needs to become? In my case, it was not even an act of forgiving, it was more an act of putting the reality into perspective and moving on.

The fact that I was politicized early helped a great deal. I realized quite early that I was not the only fatherless child in our community. I also understood that to be poor and fatherless was not my fault or the fault of my mother or sister (see *Race, Rage and Intellectual Development*). The fact of our condition was/ is related to the racial, economic, political, and social conditions of the nation. I may not have been able to articulate it at that time, but I knew that the lifestyle my family lived was quantitatively poor, oppressive, and far more restricted than that of the white family my mother cleaned house for. I also knew that color oppression led the list of those obstacles and that other restrictions generally followed: poor education, bad health care, and few employment opportunities. I knew this before I knew the language to describe it. Not eating regularly in the midst of people wasting food matures one rather quickly.

I also realized that I could spend a lifetime blaming my father for my misery and that of my sister and mother. That would not really affect him and it would stop me from seeing beyond his personhood to other reasons, just as or more important, for our condition. Therefore, I released my anger in a more fruitful and healthy way. My rites of passage were more self-induced and unplanned—nothing I would wish on my own children. My father seldom performed as a father/parent. I learned from him what *not* to do in terms of my own children and those of my extended family.

I have learned from my wife and by working with children that one can be a cultured father, be a caring man who views the healthy welfare of children as a part of one's responsibility and purpose in life. My concern about children is both a reflection and rejection of my own upbringing. I had to become an adult too early and such compressed growth and maturity can be harmful. Many of the necessary emotions of childhood, the levels and layers of intellectual and emotional development, as well as psychological and biological responses to persons and events were determined solely because of our financial, social, and racial condition. Poverty, with few if any safety nets, dictated much of my early responses to life. Too early in my life the important things were eating, having a place to live that provided adequate lights, heat and gas, having clothes to wear, and having lunch to eat at school. At ten years old, my worries were adult worries and my response to all of this was to hide my feelings and work. I have always worked. As a young boy, I did all kinds of work from collecting junk out of the alleys, paper routes, shining shoes, making brooms, setting bowling pins, doing janitorial work, and stealing, to joining the military. All of this prepared me as a man and as a father/parent.

This capacity for work and knowledge about what real work was about helped me to appreciate and respect all types of labor, especially the differences between physical and mental labor. The main reasons that I am in the "idea business" now is because of the following: (1) I recognize the developmental and economic limitations of working with one's hands and back only as well as working for others who do not care about me or my people, (2) I understand the relationship between work and power, (3) I understand how all work gives identity to workers, (4) I know that good work can be and often is creative and (5) I realize that the economic distance between professional, manager, and small business owner is not far.

Fatherhood = parenting = responsibility to the max. The critical force in the lives of healthy, developing, and creative children are parents who are healthy, developing, and creative. Fathers as nurturers understand that the major ingredients in parenting are love, family, knowledge, and resources.

Love

There are many streams of love in this large ocean that we live in. Here, I am most concerned about the love for our children. Such love is, and should be, so deep and moving that one does not have to think about putting the lives of one's children before one's own. If this exists then it seems that such care should translate into a change of life, a change of time and priorities in relationship to one's children. To love a child is to prepare a child to be better than we, the parents, are. Dr. Frances Cress Welsing has repeatedly pointed out that our children need quality "lap" time, i.e., love.

Family

I live in a three-generational family. My wife's mother lives with us. We live together not because she is dependent on us or in ill-health. We live together because she is in her mid-seventies and we all know that her need for family will increase as she grows older. We also understand that her grandchildren's need for her love, discipline and guidance is crucial at this time in their lives. The benefits in this extended family living arrangement are many:

1.   It teaches family bonding by example; we do not have to wait until a parent is ill to rearrange family living arrangements. Recreate the village in one's own family, extended family, community.

2.   A third mind, one that is thoroughly experienced in raising children, is always at hand to help.

3.   We share our experiences and resources. These may be minor, but small thing like helping to buy food or the many acts of kindness our mother showers on our children around their birthdays, graduations, and holidays are invaluable. Her constant contributions of love, labor, and resources have been immeasurable.

4.   My wife and I are both professionals and our time is valuable to others as well as to our family. This takes us away from our home and children. With our mother living in, we do not have to worry about latch-key children.

There is always a loving "parent" there to receiving them after school or play.

Knowledge

I cannot stress too much the importance of having a positive information bank. Child rearing is both traditional, new age, African-centered, and a realistic combination of all three. Intelligent parents must always be sensitive to ways in which they become more effective parents. This requires consultation with elders, professionals, and much study.

Human Resources and Bonding

The primary resources are obviously human. The type of environment we create for our children is ultimately an extension of the parents. To give children all they need, as opposed to all they want, requires money and the wise use of money. However, wise parents pull on all the resources available to them, including schools, museums, boys and girls clubs, YMCAs and YWCAs, libraries, summer camps, local colleges and universities, the arts, entertainment, and learning resources of local and state governments, churches, temples, mosques, etc. The challenge is to take advantage of all that is available in your local surroundings.

Often the father-to-son relationship is a troubling one because we fathers have not been taught how to father/parent in an effective and loving way. However, the bonding acts with our children should begin at birth. I have found in my own life that by actively participating in the birth of my children—from taking pre-birth classes to being in the bed with my wife during birth—has helped me to better appreciate and understand the birthing/bonding process.

Often what is missing in our son's lives is a father's uncritical, unconditional love. Too often we are quick to "put down" or "critique" our sons for what we think they are not doing, rather than trying to understand why they do what they do. The only way that fathers can get to the hearts of their sons is by eliminating fear in the relationship. Yes, there is a difference between fathers and sons; we are not equals. Our sons do not start out as our friends. If we nurture them properly as they grow into adults, they can become friends as well as beautiful sons. Here are some suggestions:

1. Boys need great love and environments where they feel safe. They need hands-on guidance and discipline.

2. They need to be encouraged to be the best that they can be. Constant, positive reinforcement is absolutely necessary.

3. Organized sports are great for teaching boys to work well with others, healthy competition, and the importance of team work.

4. Maintain realistic but high expectations for your son. However, the best example for this is what you do in your own life. It is always best to teach by *quiet* example.

5. Do not be afraid to show *real* affection. I kiss or hug my sons every day and most nights. Tell them often how proud you are of them and how much you love and care for them.

6. Develop a reward system for good work. This works for me with report cards. In our home, our children have weekly and daily work that they must perform. They receive a weekly allowance for this. The total amount that

I gave them for the first year, I saved half of it for them. After the year, each of my children had enough money saved to open their own savings accounts at a local bank. From that point on, one-third to one-half of the money they earned had to go into the bank. Once they were past the fifth grade, I began to reward them monetarily for their exceptional work at school. Each grading period, I would give five dollars for A's, three dollars for B's, and I would subtract one dollar for any lower grades. One-third to one-half of that money also goes into their bank accounts.

7.   Listen to your sons. If they do not abnormally fear you, they will talk to you. I found that the best way to get my sons to talk about their problems with me is to go on walks together. I or they initiate a walk at any time.

8.   Always question yourself as a father/parent. Try to "objectively" look at your own actions, and do not be afraid to admit mistakes and failures in your child-rearing efforts. It is best to stop and reverse that which is not working than to prolong ineffective parenting. Reassessment is always necessary. A good question to ask yourself is, "What are my shortcomings as a father/parent?" Often you can not answer that question. Ask your wife-mate or another family member close to your situation for help in seeing yourself in a more realistic light.

9.   Definitions of "manhood" or "maleness" are in a state of flux. However, the one definition that does not change is being responsible. Provide for the needs of your children. Pass on developmental values to your children. Put your children's needs before your own needs.

10. Teach them that violence is not the answer to conflict resolution. Teach them that there is a profound difference between violence and aggression. Meaningless violence in the home, on the streets, or in the schools is, without exception, unnecessary. However, certain types aggression are legitimate. Violence to protect one's personhood from the violent act of others is allowed and encouraged. One has to be aggressive in this world if one is to succeed at most activities. One cannot compete and succeed in any number of life activities without healthy aggression. Seldom does aggression in business, studies, or sports lead to violence. Remember, to compete is to be aggressive, not violent.

11. Show your sons by example how to relate to women. Obviously, the best example would be your relationship to their mother. I have written extensively about this in other books.* We men must always be willing to check ourselves on our outdated definition of women as wives, mothers, parents, providers, workers, and lovers. Early in our son's lives, we must begin to talk about sex and love with them. We must introduce them in a healthy way to the role of men as lovers and sexual partners. This is extremely difficult, but it must be done! Fathering children does not make one a man. Manhood and fatherhood carries with it responsibility to oneself, one's community, and one's children.

12. Always try to introduce them to the real world. For

In my book *Black Men: Obsolete, Single and Dangerous? The African American Family in Transition*, I write about this subject in greater detail.

example, your teenage son after earning his driver's license may want to drive alone. It is your responsibility to prepare him for any and all negative possibilities. What is he to do if stopped by the police? His actions may save his life and you pain. If stopped, (a) sit in the car with hands on steering wheel or slowly get out of the car and keep hands where they can be seen, (b) speak in an intelligent manner, without referring to wisecracks, (c) do what the officer asks you to do, and (d) if there is a problem, settle it later with family and lawyer present.

I often state that racism is not only alive and well, it is a growth industry. My answer to fathers/parents and sons is that this fact needs to be a part of each person's working reality. Our children should understand the debilitating effects of racism, but not allow it to stop them from developing. That is why we parents are there to guide them through this minefield. The question is, how do we neutralize racism as we actualize our own worldview? A better question is—do you/we have a worldview that is not an abridged copy of the one that now stops too many of us in our tracks? Our children must understand that a better world cannot be built on criticism alone. We must be about the building of a world that is life-giving and life-saving. This building requires work, study, family development, political involvement, economic planning, and vision.

The fact that we are Black and people of African descent first is a positive one and must be used wisely. The world is often a cold, difficult place that is not about taking care of those who do not work to take care of themselves. We must teach our children to carry themselves in a dignified, honorable, and self-protective way, and teach them to always remember: if somebody gives you something, they can always take it away. We must purge from our minds this dependency, welfare, beggar mentality, and teach and show our children in an earthbound manner, how self-reliance is not only possible, but necessary for Black development in the 21st century.

To this end, as a culturally focused, politically aware, production-oriented, responsible and loving father/parent, I *must* be—along with my wife—the major influence on our children. This means that regardless of what is happening on the street, in schools, in film, on television, on the basketball courts, or football field, we are, in consultation with our children, the final word on the values practiced in our lives. Our children also understand that the time will come for them to run their own lives, but that for now they are in a learning and dependency mode. Each year of productive growth increasingly liberates them. Responsible acts, plus age, brings privileges.

Finally, what I have tried to be to my children is not only a father/parent they can touch, relate to, understand, and feel, but a hero in their eyes. When my son chose to write about me as the hero in his life for a school term paper, I knew that all my work and sacrifice had been worth the effort. Our goal to be the fathers that they respect, love, and yes, understand. But first, before we even arrive at this special point, our children will always be testing us. The crucial test is that we have to be there for them, frequently.

STANDING AS AN AFRICAN MAN

Black Men in a Sea of Whiteness

Where do I belong and what is the price I have to pay for being where and who I am?

Study the faces of children that look like you. Walk your streets, count the smiles and bright eyes, and make a mental note of their ages. At what age do our children cease to smile naturally, smile full-teeth, uninhibited, expecting full life? At what age will memory of lost friends, and lost relatives, deaden their eyes? Where does childhood stop in much of our community? At seven, eight? How many killings, rapes, beatings, verbal and mental abuse, hustles, get over programs, drug infestations, drive-by shootings/drive-by leaders must they witness before their eyes dry up for good and their only thought is: "Will I make it to the age of twenty-five?" When the life in the eyes of our children do not gleam brightly with future and hope, we cease being nurturers and become repairers of broken spirits and stolen souls. This is the state we are now in and too often it is too late.

Where do I belong and what is the price I have to pay for being where and who I am?

If you don't know, you can't do.

Who do we buy our food from? Who do we rent our

apartments from? Who do we buy our clothes, furniture, cars, and life bettering needs from? Whose land do we walk, sleep, live, play, work, get high, chase women, lie, steal, produce children and die on? Why is it that 800,000 Black men and 50,000 Black women populated the nation's prisons? Is race a factor in a land where white people control most things of value? Is race a factor in a county where young Black boys and men are dying quicker than their birth rate? When do we declare war on our own destruction? Why is it that the Blacker one is the worse it is? Who taught Black people that killing Black people is all right and sometimes honorable?

This is Our Charge!

Study the landscape. Read the music in your hearts. Remember the beauty of mothers, sisters, and the women in our lives that talked good about us. Remember when we talked good about us. Remember when we talked good about them. Understand the importance of ideas.

This is Our Mission!

Pick up a book. Challenge the you in you. Rise above the limited expectations of people who do not like you and never will like you. Rise above the self-hatred that slowly eats your heart, mind, and spirit away. Find like-minded brothers. Study together. Talk together. Find each others hearts. Ask the right questions. Why are we poor? Why are our children not educated? Why are our children dying at such an unbelievable rate? Why are we landless? What does land ownership have to do with race? What does wealth have to do with race? Why do we hate being called African and Black? What does Africa mean to me, us? Why is Africa in a state of confusion and civil war? Why is there no work in our communities? What is the difference between a producer and a consumer? What do we produce that is sold and used world-wide? Whose knowledge is most valuable for the development of Black (African) people? Would I kill myself and others that look like me if I loved myself and those that look like me? Where does self-love come from? Who taught me, us, self-hatred? Is self-hatred an idea? Is self-love an idea? Whose ideas do we tap-dance to? Whose ideas do we impress each other with? Are African (Black) ideas crucial to our discourse and development? Can a Black person be multi-cultural if he/she does not have his/her culture first? When do we declare war on ignorance, intellectual betrayal, self-destruction, pimpism, weakening pleasures, European worldviews, beggar mentalities, and white world supremacy? Is race an idea? When will we use the race idea to benefit us?

Where do I belong and what is the price I have to pay for being where and who I am?

We belong among the people worldwide that look like us. We belong to a world where we produce rather than consume. We belong to a world where the measurement of Black beauty and worth is internal and cultural.

We belong where our education is not anti-us.

We belong among African men who are brothers and brothers who are Africans. How will we recognize them?

You will recognize your brothers
by the way they act and move throughout the world.
there will be a strange force about them,
there will be unspoken answers in them.
this will be obvious not only to you but to many.

the confidence they have in themselves and in
their people will be evident in their quiet saneness.
the way they relate to women will be
clean, complementary, responsible, with honesty and as partners.
the way they relate to children will be
strong and soft full of positive direction and as example.
the way they relate to men
will be that of questioning our position in this world,
will be one of planning for movement and change,
will be one of working for their people,
will be one of gaining and maintaining trust within the culture.
these men at first will seem strange and unusual but
this will not be the case for long.
they will train others and the discipline they display
will become a way of life for many.
they know that this is difficult
but this is the life that they have chosen
for themselves, for us, for life:
they will be the examples,
they will be the answers,
they will be the first line builders,
they will be the creators,
they will be the first to give up the weakening pleasures,
they will be the first to share a black value system,
they will be the workers,
they will be the scholars,
they will be the providers,
they will be the historians,
they will be the doctors, lawyers, farmers, priests
and all that is needed for development and growth.
you will recognize these brothers
and
they will not betray you.

WHITE PEOPLE ARE PEOPLE TOO

*(For Mead, Hillman, Bly, Densmore and
Multi-cultural Men's Work)*

Most struggles have a way of homogenizing people,
of devaluing individuality
always looking at the big suffering revolutionary picture,
our pains inhibit seeing beyond our struggle,
beyond culture, beyond race.

race struggle can be cleansing and uplifting,
race struggle can be blinding and self-righteous,
race struggle seldom separates the evil from the ignorant,
> *"bad and not so bad, good and not so good, best and*
> *better,"*
race struggle minimizes intra-race struggle.

parts of a lifetime are lost documenting the enemy.
in struggle
we only know each other and
each other is not the world

it is not in me to love an enemy
who has committed horrific crimes against children.
are crimes transferrable?
are crimes inherited by sons and daughters
who reject that history
and work for reconciliation and reparations?

*can being Black and African-centered guide me to the
centering best of Asians, Europeans, Native Americans,
indigenous peoples, women, others?*

*it is in me to grow.
to walk among vegetation and cultures, to think.
it is in me to see that pain is colorless
it is in me to value the differences of others.*

*It is human to share,
I am not suicidal.*

WHO OWNS THE EARTH?

NEW WORLD ORDER

Language, Ideas and War

Racism has been described as the American metaphor; more often than not, it has been a nightmare for its victims. As we make ready to enter the 21st century, we are no closer to solving this international problem than we were when W. E. B. Du Bois gave us his insights of it in the earlier part of this century. My generation grew up in the fire of clearer definitions. Racism, i.e., white world supremacy, is now understood by many people of color worldwide as a European aberration that has wreaked havoc on most cultures.

A misreading or misinterpretation of an enemy's motives and actions can lead to intellectual fuzziness and historical "whiteout." Historical memory is absolutely necessary for any people. However, to a people who are trapped in the historical paradigm of its conqueror, such memory is essential. We live in difficult and dangerous times and if nothing else, accurate history is a major element in psychological protection.

History can also represent insightful direction because the past often reveals secrets to the future. For example, if all Black children were introduced to the history or culture of our people beyond an "enslaved" context, maybe their view of themselves would rise above the limited expectations of others and themselves. By no means is this an idle assumption. Historical memory that stresses creativity and building values, economic productivity, ownership, and winning rather than dependency and childish consumption has bred a good number of American whites to come out winners even when the win is questionable and of little historical significance, such as Desert Storm. This kind of nurturing can mean the big difference in the psychological feeling and development of a people. That the homecoming parades that followed Desert Storm were longer than the war itself is a serious comment on the historical context and nature of American political and military realities.

As I watched President Bush act and lie his way through his 1991 State of the Union address, I was reminded of his mentor Ronald Reagan. I was also reminded of the 1990 Civil Rights Bill that he vetoed and the African-American men and women who served as thirty percent of the front line troops in the Persian Gulf. All of a sudden, Mr. Bush was eager to consider a new Civil Rights Bill as long as Black men and women, whose enlistment in the all-volunteer army is almost three times their population representation in the nation as a whole (twelve percent), are willing to engage his and his friends' enemies.

George Bush, his cabinet, and a weak-kneed, acquiescent Congress carried us into a war that responsible men and women considered insane, irrational, and racist. The short-memory people do not recall that for the last ten years preceding that war Iraq and Saddam Hussein were allies of the United States. This country supplied Iraq with "intelligence" and food in its eight year war against Iran and looked the other way when Saddam Hussein gassed the minorities in his own population. Few remember the U.S. ambassador to Iraq, April Glaspie, giving

Saddam Hussein the "thumbs-up" to settle his dispute with Kuwait, basically stating that it was an Arab problem.

Bush needed a crisis to save him from the domestic and economic quicksand that was swallowing him. In less than six months, this country and its nine European, Japanese, and Arab allies deployed over one-half million troops and millions of tons of weapon systems and equipment to Saudi Arabia. By December 1990, George Bush had declared that the embargo against Iraq was ineffective in removing Saddam Hussein from Kuwait. He intensified the greasing of palms, arm twisting, and deal making in the U.N. Security Council, and Desert Shield became Desert Storm. After the "victories" of Grenada and Panama, Saddam Hussein gave Bush another Third World War that he could easily sell to the American people. All the ingredients were there: oil, a ruthless nonwhite dictator, an anti-Christ Muslim, an enemy of Israel, a "madman" with chemical and nuclear weapons capacity, and a zealous one-half million man army looking for a fight. Welcome to the first 21st century war, via CNN's window to Iraq and Kuwait. The first Nintendo war.

The hypocrisy of U.S. foreign policy is an insult to intelligent people. Why was there no such urgency around the struggle of South African Blacks? Why didn't this country move militarily around the invasion and destruction of Lebanon and the deaths of hundred of marines? What about Israel and its occupation of the West Bank and the Gaza Strip for the last twenty years? What about Reagan's, Bush's, and the CIA's backing of the Contras in the destabilization and destruction of Nicaragua? Ever since Europe's War on the World Number II, the U.S. and its brothers have only fought people of color. This country's attack on Iraq had very little to do with the liberation of Kuwait; rather, it was about oil and White world hegemony.

The war was in keeping with the West's intolerance and hatred for people of color who refuse to imitate and kowtow to them and for any religion that challenges the Christian-Judeo philosophy of life. Surely Islam, and its emerging influence in the world, has enraged and struck fear into the hearts of many of the proponents of Christianity and Judaism. And, of course, leave it to Bush, the Willie Horton President, to personalize this conflict.

In December 1990, George Bush, blowing steam to some visiting Congressmen, stated: "If we get into an armed situation" with Saddam Hussein, "he's going to get his ass kicked." And, Saddam Hussein, who has his own evil identity, became, in the words of the most powerful military man in the world, not just a Third World dictator, but the live reincarnation of Hitler. Why do so many Americans believe this racist nonsense?

Without serious debate or argument, thought becomes lazy and polluted. The ignorance that exists among the populace in the United States can be attributed partially to the demise of serious political debate. Also, the failure of print and electronic media to serve as carriers of serious analysis and the uncritical acceptance of most reportage as correct and accurate has contributed to this mindset. The inability of many people to distinguish the public relations strategy of a politician or commercial product from the truth is not a great concern for the majority of citizens in this land. However, such ignorance and naivete is at the core of our problem and is not simply another discussion for "pin-head" intellectuals.

Any people who do not critically question the state of the

world are a people doomed to the back lots of other people's realities. Language, like most things in a market-driven economy, can be corrupted. Languages, which are spoken and written images, can be packaged for, directed toward, and assimilated into almost any community. Language and the images it produces are the life-line of popular culture. The language of mass culture is communicated via business, education, politics, healthcare, religion, law, crime, sports, entertainment, and war. Its power to inform or confuse should not be underestimated. The language George Bush, Dick Cheney, and Colin Powell used to sell the people this war was the same language that pushed this country into Vietnam, Grenada, and Panama: the language of deception, childlike patriotism, and disrespect.

The military spends millions studying persuasion in language research. All industries have their own double-speak and clarity-avoidance. Bush as Commander-in-Chief via the CIA, United Nations Representative, and Vice President is at the top of his game in truth dodging. So rather than killed or wasted, the enemy is neutralized. To keep young minds positive one engages in CBM—Confidence Building Measures. Bombs are "ordinances," and tanks, planes and other weapons of war are part of "weapon systems." The war was not about the defeat of Iraq but the "liberation of Kuwait." Generals used maps and video screens or explain "successes" while news people asked prescripted questions, laughed, and clapped. All this obscures clear thinking and keeps the mind away from the reality of war: death, destruction and monumental suffering.

And what of the press with its noncritical, flag-waving, unfair coverage of the "Arab" side of this conflict? Most of the reporters acted like gung-ho teenage troops in the field; they seemed to be looking for battle ribbons to show off back home to aid them in future promotions after Iraq had been bombed into the sand to rot. The excitement for most was over being there, not telling the truth or digging for the real reasons for the war.

What little background the public received was Pentagon-packaged or rewritten to fit the condensed prose of *Time*, *Newsweek,* and *U.S.A. Today*. The popular press did not present any serious Arab or Arab American commentary to give the Arab/Palestinian side of this war. With the possible exception of the *Nation*, the *Progressive*, *In These Times*, National Public Radio, and a few other independent journals and newspapers, the Arabs, (new niggers), were all but invisible. Sounds like business as usual.

However, the Israeli solution to "the problem" commanded front page coverage and evening news highlights daily—from New York's Mayor Dinkin's praying at Jerusalem's Wailing Wall to the racist utterings of A.M. Rosenthal and William Safire in the *New York Times*. The Jewish side of this struggle was never without heroes, potential big dollars, and constant historical rewriting. The press' acceptance of the "nonlinkage" connection as pushed by Bush and Israel defied reality. This is not to deny the outright opportunism and murderous actions of Saddam Hussein in this invasion of Kuwait or his invasion of Iran ten years ago. However, to deny that this entire Middle East scenario had nothing to do with the Jewish occupation of Palestine is to Stalinize history, to white-out the last fifty years. Did the Six-Day War, or what the Arabs call the Defeat of Hazieran 5, happen? We African Americans have our own difficulties with Arabs, but that does not negate history, nor does it lessen our empathy for their suffering at the hands of the West or their own people. Why didn't Ted Koppel hold a town hall meeting (similar to the Nelson Mandela program) with Edward Said, one of the few Arab voices not buckdancing to the music of Saddam Hussein or George Bush? It's difficult to double-talk with individuals who are not looking to advance themselves but to serve as learned spokesperson for their people.

What are the other obscene realities of Bush's war that were relegated to the sidelines and back pages of newspapers?

1. The country was distracted from scandals like the Savings and Loans debacle. This one trillion dollar (and growing) rip-off allowed Bush's son, Neil, some congressmen and several other well-connected white men to walk away free, rich, and smiling with an American flag in one hand and their sons and daughters going to the best private schools money can buy.

2. The national debt, four trillion dollars and rising, needed a war like Black people need more poverty. It is estimated that the Gulf War cost the American people over one billion dollars a day, even with the contributions from the allies.

3. Homelessness and unemployment are at unmanageable levels. One of the reasons that the armed forces are overpopulated with African Americans, Latinos, Native Americans, women, and poor whites is because they could not find employment opportunities in the civilian world. Many joined the military as a way out of poverty and a chance for advancement and a possible college education. The families of reservists who least expected to be called

especially suffered.

4. The infrastructures of the country are falling apart, especially in urban areas. Sewer systems and water filtration plants are old and overworked. Unusable bridges populate the land. The ineffectiveness of the nation's rail system is a disgrace for an industrialized country.

5. Tens of millions of Americans do not have adequate health care coverage. AIDS continues to spread like polluted water, affecting mainly African American women, and illegal drugs are as available as rock candy.

6. The prisons are overpopulated with African American and Latino men. There are more Black men in prison than in the nation's colleges and universities. Black men are forever at war, whether in the Middle East or in the streets of America (e.g., the Los Angeles rebellions).

7. The FDIC is close to insolvent. This crisis guarantees the failure of hundreds of banks. The insurance industry and the real estate market border on collapse. Bankruptcy and Chapter 11 filings are at an all-time high. Michigan, Massachusetts, New York, Pennsylvania, and other states are crying broke.

8. The environment has been compromised by man-made disasters, such as the greenhouse effect and oil spillings. This country's environmental policy is nonexistent. The oil spilled from the bombed wells in the Gulf will take years, decades, to correct itself. This country has no serious energy policy, which is why oil—a major pollutant—is critically important to this waste-oriented

economy. As a result, conservation takes a back seat to immature consumerism.

9. Institutional and individual white supremacy (racism), which poisons and imprisons everything it touches, is a growth industry in America and the world.

I could go on, but I am sure that by now you understand how Bush and his sidekicks truly betrayed the American people. Bush, his family, and the Congress ran from the hard and honorable task of rebuilding the economy. They purported to support Saudi Arabia, a country that is ruled by a corrupt family that still has slaves; they demanded the "liberation" of another corrupt, family-run country (Kuwait), whose only importance is that it sits on vast oil reserves; they turned Saddam Hussein into an Arab hero who is now revered by the same people he once abused and killed; and they have allowed Israel to side-step the legitimate concerns of the Palestinian people. All of this and more intensified while the Saudis grew richer by the second, and Japan and Germany re-worked the world's economic map.

Now that much of the shooting war in the Middle East is confined to Iraqis shooting each other, the Emir of Kuwait and his family have resumed business as usual, the Israelis have built another layer of concrete around their brains, the Palestinians continue to grapple with inept leadership and negative Western press, and the U.S. troops have returned as conquering heroes having fought a mirage of an enemy, (inflicting tens of thousands of civilian casualties). Will the truth ever be told?

For Bush and his people to emphatically state that the war was fought for the "liberation of Kuwait" (as if Kuwait resembles anything close to a democracy) was scandalous. This country deployed personnel and material to the Middle East to protect other people's assets and Western interest in them (oil). Kuwait's huge investment in the West reveals the depth of its involvement. (According to the *Wall Street Journal* 11 March 1991, "10% of Britain's Midland Bank PLC, 14% of Germany's Daimler-Bez Ag, and all of Sante Fe International Corp. of the U.S.") Israel's encouragement of U.S. military intervention almost equalled the insanity and stupidity of Saddam Hussein's exhortations about his "invincible" armed forces.

Hopefully, history will sort this mess out, but that says little for the loss of life and suffering that took place. Yes, it is good that so few young U.S. men and women were killed or hurt, but what did these high tech "heroes" come home to? How will their consciences play out once they begin to ponder the death and carnage they left behind? It seems to me that the same old group got over. United States contractors and their Western allies will rebuild Kuwait, and maybe eventually Iraq, to the sum of $100 billion or more. The arms industry gained immensely in research and promises of new sales to the Saudis and Kuwaitis. The United States reasserted its influence in the region while backing the Israelis without question.

This affair is a sad lesson for young people in the United States. This country's government has lost all semblance of moral or political credibility among Arabs and others. In terms of damage to civilians, environment and the infrastructure of both countries, the Persian Gulf War should be a source of shame to all involved. The other losses are reason, national debate, international dialogue, UN credibility, and the chance to affect real change in the outlaw mentalities that run the world.

Money: Its Uses, Misuses

and Why the Vast Majority of Us Don't Have Any

One does not have to be Adam Smith, John Maynard Keynes, Karl Marx, Robert Heilbroner, or John Kenneth Galbraith to understand that the international and most national economies are not working for the great majority of people. In my youth, Marxism was the answer to heaven on earth. At best, a Marxist analysis is helpful in understanding the inequities in market economies. It is not the answer to the powerful pull of capitalism and the embarrassing downfall and failure of Communism in Eastern Europe.

Economics is a foreign subject to most of us, myself included. Yet, as a poet-businessman, I have had to soil and wash my hands because every two weeks my co-workers do not want a poem but a check for their labor. To state categorically that I understand the "art" of making money is to infer a falsehood that I most readily admit to. My understanding of market economies is about as substantive as my reflections on quantum physics or any math beyond algebra.

However, I have always possessed a deep desire to be independent of people who do not like me, especially those who have a history of murdering for profit, power, and deep-seated racist beliefs. Due to the poet, politics, and color in me, I will never be a major player in the money game. It is not that money does not interest me; it does, but there are many more important concerns that take up what little time I have outside of writing, working, and studying—such as family and extended family development, teaching, editing, publishing, and maintaining my health and moral state of mind. I believe it extremely unhealthy and unethical to misuse, exploit, or take advantage of any people for personal or "collective" profit. There are many, many acts that I will not perform for money or wealth.

However, there are many ideas about general wealth and power that even someone as ignorant of the field as I am cannot miss:

1.   The making of a great deal of money is not a fair game, nor is it open to all who may understand best how to use it. Money making is not an equal opportunity employer.

2.   Very few people who work for a living will ever have any serious money, this includes managers and small business owners. If one works for a weekly check, he or she will probably not be able to save enough money to move into the investment class, where one's money works for one, rather than one working for money.

3.   People with big money generally have had some help: (a) inherited wealth; (b) stolen wealth; (c) idea wealth, yours or somebody else's; (d) entertainment wealth—tap dancing on the art of other people; (e) retail wealth—Walmart/ Sam's Club; (f) real estate wealth—building Disneylands and strip malls on all the farm lands available; (g) advertising wealth—the key is to sell to as many people as possible objects that they do not need or want; (h.) Law firm wealth—finding the loop holes to keep the money

with the people who have money; (i) investment wealth—avoid junk bonds and men like Michael Milken and Ivan Boesky (j) sports wealth—be like Mike and men like him; and (k) media wealth—to make us think that the Mikes are major players in the wealth game and, that you too can be rich (that's why lotteries exist).

4. One of the reasons capitalism works in America is that most people do not realize that it does not work. The great secret is that there is socialism for the rich, near rich, and recent Pentagon graduates. For wanna-be lobbyists, the best experience on a resume is "former Congressman." The incestuous relationship between government and business is obscene. Who you know and what you know about them is as important as having a good lawyer. For example, that much of the large farming is subsidized in America says a lot about power and political friendships. Few would call a farmer lazy or nonproductive (that does not explain why small family farms are going the way of the dinosaur). However, the subsidizing for the dairy and tobacco farms would put most "welfare queens" to shame. The waste in the federal budget could possibly finance several small nations into the next millennium with some change left over.

5. People with big hearts do not have money. That is why foundations and grant-giving agencies are named for and financed by the fortunes of dead men. Men like the Rockefellers, Morgans, Fords and others built their wealth on the bodies of others. Foundations were created by their families and friends to give some of the "blood money"

away in order to help create positive memories of them.

6.   The greed factor in a capitalist economy is the fuel that runs the engine and cannot be underestimated. When people love money first and foremost, children generally suffer. The people who take economic risks against unhealthy odds do not understand the game. Big capitalism is risky, yes. But the winners are always those inside the loop who have the inside track on the next trade. However, for the middle player, capitalism is like a lottery game. Often, it is a roll of the dice or fall of the ball. The higher one is in the game, the fewer the balls one has to contend with. After all, the higher-ups are generally making the balls and machines that operate the game.

7.   The saying that "it takes money to make money" is a truism that is timeless in most cultures. Also, there is the saying, "nothing is parted quicker than a fool and his money." Most people with serious money do not buy lottery tickets, gamble on riverboats, or wager on horse races, sports games, or prize fights. The seriously rich own riverboats, sports teams, race tracks and horses, boxers, and the hotels where the middle class and poor can stay in comfort while they lose their underwear.

8.   The reality that "money makes money" means that most people, and I do mean literally the great majority of the world's people—Black, White, Red, Brown, and Yellow—will not be able to join the monied class. Most rich people keep their secrets to themselves and do not welcome new members without a great deal of consideration and investigation.

9. You can always tell who the people are without money. They generally wear overpriced, poorly made clothes that are valued more for their label than for the quality. Many drive expensive cars that cost one-half of their yearly salary and carry large amounts of money around with them. People who have real money keep it to themselves because they do not want most of us to know about it for obvious reasons: (a) they think that we may ask/beg for some; (b) they think that we may try to steal it from them; (c) all kinds of charitable and not-for-profit groups would be camping on their doorstep; and (d) it may attract too many reporters who write for the *Nation*, the *Progressive,* and *Mother Jones*.

10. Ask a family member to explain NAFTA (North American Free Trade Agreement) and GATT (General Agreement on Tariffs and Trade) to you. If they do not know, try to explain it to them. If ignorance is victorious, call a Congress person and really get confused. Just remember, the first rule of NAFTA and GATT: someone is going to make BIG money, and it won't be you. Oh, here are some more letters that you need to think about, BCCI (Bank of Commerce and Credit International).

For too many people, money is a religion. To be a priest in its church you have to love money more than people. As a political poet-writer-artist, I have never made any real money. The most money I have ever had at any given time was the $12,000 I received from an NEA (National Endowment for the Arts) fellowship, and that lasted about two months. I have given away more money than I have saved, primarily to agencies serving children; I have invested the majority of the money I have made into the Institute of Positive Education, Third World Press, the African American Book Center, *Black Books Bulletin,* and other Black organizations struggling for human rights. Everything else has gone to my children—to their livelihood and education—and to "Uncle Sam." With two daughters currently in college and two sons waiting in the wings, I am sure I will be working for the rest of my life.

I will never forget my son questioning me about the salaries of highly paid baseball and basketball players (mainly the Black ones.) He had heard, obviously from a poorly paid sports announcer belittling the motives of such players, that if they are paid much more it will destroy the game. I asked my son to think about these points: (1) who signs the checks of the players; (2) how much money do the check signers make; and (3) as long as new teams are created, old players retire and the public can relive their own childhood through sports, the games will survive, and the players will never be compensated at the same level as the owners.

What Should Money-less People Do?

Part of our dilemma is that many of us do not understand the value of family, extended family, and community in relationship to wealth. I have always felt that family is as important as participating in a quality pension plan. Therefore, very human relationships, built around life-giving, life-saving, and life-sustaining values, are a crucial part of the bottom line for a healthy life.

This can be translated in a number of ways:

1. Black churches have always been secondary homes for

most of us. Where is the "wealth" of the church—which is a collective wealth—being invested? It should be invested back into the community it serves in any number of ways, including (a) credit unions, (b) food co-ops, (c) rehabilitating and building of new homes in their communities, (d) elderly apartments, (e) restaurants with low-cost, high-quality food, (f) chain grocery stores using local farmers as a base, (g) bulk buying of the items the church members use the most (e.g., stoves, refrigerators, etc.), (h) children-centered activities (e.g., after-school programs, boys and girls clubs, etc.), (i) whatever we need, we should be able to buy in our own communities and therefore recirculate the money.

2. Support a national Black bank. African American are 35 million strong in this country. If the 18 million adults among us put one dollar per week in a national bank, there is great potential for re-investment and growth. Part of the problem here is, who would we trust to administer $18 million a week of our money? This is a moral/value problem. A trust problem.

3. Do not be afraid of starting small businesses. This country was built on the backs of indigenous people, the backs of enslaved Africans and indentured Asians, Latinos, and Europeans. Small businesses still employ the majority of the people. We have to get into the business of business. Our children need to be nurtured and educated in the self-reliant occupations. While it is true that we must make a profit, we must never lose sight of the human side of the equation. If we have to work for large multi-national

corporations, we must never forget who we are. In fact, Black folks must become guerrilla warriors in the board-rooms, state buildings, universities, and playing fields of the business world. We must work, often undercover to bring more quality Blacks into our work places. That is what culturally focused guerrilla warriors do; they help their own as they fight against evil.

4. Support small farmers. Local farmers need us and we need them. Part of our health problems could be minimized if we had fresh food. The closer the crop is to the market, the better it is for the consumer. What about the Black rural-urban connection?

5. Organize and study. Work with like-minded people. Practice good values. Oppose all forms of greed. Teach our children frugality and productive skills. Do not be afraid to fight big-monied interests, whether private or governmental.

6. In a highly competitive world, ideas about increasing efficiency and quality, while cutting costs to maintain and develop one's business, are critical. Fifteen years ago, Federal Express, Kinkos, personal and business fax ma-chines and personal computers were just ideas. Today, we do not know how we got along without them. Black colleges and universities with business schools should think of ways to make the community that surrounds them empowerment zones. How can professors and students take the classroom to the streets and revitalize at least the neighborhoods nearby.

7. Most of the mom and pop stores in Black communities in

urban areas are owned and controlled by other cultures—primarily Arabs and Koreans. They use a families and extended families system, which is financed internally. It is something like a tri-circle:

The middle circle represents old line families or new families with money. They loan money to the second circle of families who have been here for a while and worked their way up from retail to distribution. The third circle represents the new arrivals and/or poor of the Arabs, Koreans, and other cultures. They borrow money from the center at very low interest (3-5%) and buy retail storefronts and go head to head with Black businesses. The center circle family loans the money to the third circle family on the condition that they (a) buy their products from the second circle family who are distributors, (b) employ mainly family and extended family only, (c) help to develop the third circle concept and (d) keep outsiders out.

8. The ultimate goal is for our culture to control at least a sector of the national economy. If we supply fruit,

vegetables, a specific labor market, or shoe strings to the nation we would be in much better shape than we are now. Our consumer dollars need to be directed only to those businesses that support us by (a) employment, (b) supporting our service organizations and institutions, (c) invest their resources in our businesses and communities, (d) consider our ideas in their own development.

9. Move to control the real estate in our communities with a strategy of going beyond the African American community. This work entails new buildings starts and rehabs. Black people who are architects, construction workers, contractors, suppliers should be involved in all the construction that takes place in African American communities.

10. We have to be mindful of the global economy with a special eye on Africa. In too many of the future economic forecasts, Africa is not even considered as a viable player at the conservation or investment levels. (See *the West, Africa, and the New Millennium.*)

When we consider the world's population in its relationship to usable land and water, any thinking person can see that we are in trouble. Everything of value that we need in order to maintain a quality life comes from land and water. Conscientious people, groups, organizations, churches, etc., need to buy land and maintain it. There is something about living close to the land and water that enables one to maintain a more human perspective. Here is a list of books that I think may help as you reconsider the world we live in.

References

Bartlett Donald L. and James B. Steele. *America: What Went Wrong?* (Kansas City: Andrews and McMeel), 1993.
_____. *America: Who Really Pays the Taxes* (Kansas City: Andrews and McMeel), 1994.

Berry, Wendell. *Sex, Economy, Freedom and Community* (New York: Pantheon), 1993.

Brown, Lester R. (ed.) *State of the World* (New York: W. W. Norton and Co.), 1993.

Caplan, Lincoln. *Skadden: Power, Money and the Rise of a Legal Empire* (New York: Farrar, Straus and Giroux), 1993.

Chomsky, Noam. *Year 501: The Conquest Continues* (Boston: South End Press), 1993.

Galbraith, John K. *The Culture of Contentment* (Boston: Houghton Mifflin Co.), 1992.

Greider, William. *Who will Tell the People: The Betrayal of American Democracy* (New York: Simon and Schuster), 1992.

Heilbrener, Robert L. *An Inquiry into the Human Prospect* (New York: W. W. Norton & Co.), 1974.

Hitchens, Christopher. *Blood, Class and Nostalgia* (New York: Farrar, Straus and Giroux), 1990.

Lapham, Lewis H. *Money and Class in America* (New York: Weidenfeld and Nicolson), 1988.

Needleman, Jacob. *Money and the Meaning of Life* (New York: Doubleday Currency) 1991.

Paepke, C. Owen. *The Evolution of Progress* (New York: Random House), 1993.

Roszak, Theodore. *The Voice of the Earth* (New York: Simon and Schuster), 1992.

Stein, Benjamin J. *A License to Steal*, (New York: Simon and Schuster), 1992.

Stewart, James B. *Den of Thieves* (New York: Simon and Schuster), 1991.

Thompson, William Irwin. *The American Replacement of Nature* (New York: Doubleday Currency), 1991.

State of the World, 1993 - a yearly report of the Worldwatch
    Institute.

Periodicals—Newspapers
The Nation
Mother Jones
The Progressive
Z Magazine
The Black Scholar
Black Enterprise
Black Books Bulletin
Forbes
the New York Times
the Washington Post
the Wallstreet Journal

THE WEST,
AFRICA, AND THE NEW MILLENNIUM

H ow does Africa and its people fit into world politics and
economics as we enter the new century? Will we be beggars
or buyers, producers or consumers, land owners, or renters?
Will we be major players in the world of finance, communica-
tions, technology, biology, genetics, information, and agriculture? Will we be weak-minded imitators, grateful to be able to
spend our resources on the economic development of others?
Who owns Africa? In this post colonialist world, has Africa
moved any closer to becoming self-reliant and a net exporter of
goods and services rather than an importer of mostly everything, including ideas?

As South Africa completes its first all-race election, Nigeria can not seem to have an election without invalidating the
results. Haiti and Somalia continue to dismantle themselves in
the corruption of their leadership, the desperation of their
people, and neglect and poor policies of the world community.
While the former USSR (now Russia) struggles to reposition
itself on the world stage, its former nation-states blow each
other up, and the European community reorganizes and positions itself for the next millennium. Simultaneously, Asia,
under the leadership of China, Japan, and Korea, braces itself
for GATT (General Agreement on and Tariffs and Trade) and

each other. While Mexico tries to explain the "benefits" of NAFTA (North America Free Trade Agreement) to its people, the Serbs and the Rwandans practice "ethnic cleansing" under the watchful eyes of many who view it as population control. Anyway, who gives a damn? It is all too complicated—let's all go out for ribs, pizza, and beer and leave the thinking and running of the world to others.

It is clear that the world is changing. That the great majority of the world's people will only be pawns in this gigantic chess game indicates how peripheral most of us are to the decisions made that will affect our lives and those of our children. Over the last few years, European and American scholars, writers, foreign policy experts, and practitioners have been holding conferences, and debating in their journals and books the significance of the "New World Order." The new global tensions, according to some of their thinking, will no longer be state-to-state conflicts but the confrontation of civilizations, the clash of cultures. These cultures are broadly defined entities that share history, psychology, language, ethnicity, race, memory, and religion.

Samuel P. Huntington in his essay "The Clash of Civilizations?" (*Foreign Affairs*, Summer 1993) contributes to the national debate. The publication of *Preparing for the Twenty-First Century* by Paul Kennedy was favorably received by most journals and newspaper as a blue-print for the West. Robert D. Kaplans's "The Coming Anarchy" (*Atlantic Monthly*, February 1994) offers a view of a world in which we better arm ourselves. *Tribes*, by Joel Kotkin argues rather persuasively that the new centers of power and wealth will continue to be in the hands of Jews, British/Americans, Japanese, Chinese, and

Indians. Not to be outdone, the left weighed in with a very important analysis in the August 1993 issue of the *New Internationalist (NI)*, "The New Globalism." Their position is that the same old gang (multinational companies in their "stateless" fight for profit) will wheel and deal and checkmate each other. Noam Chomsky confirms the United States role as a major player in the future with a devastating analysis of its past and present in his books *Year 501: The Conquest Continues* and *The Prosperous Few and the Restless Many*.

The two common trends that emerge from much of the data is that (1) the West will maintain its economic, political, and military dominance with the East under the leadership of China, Japan, and India going toe-to-toe for ultimate leadership and power; (2) Africa (primarily sub-Saharan Africa) will be the big loser on the world stage as we enter the 21st century. This is not surprising if one has been reading the literature and listening to the leadership. As the evening news and morning headlines stress the carnage in Bosnia and Rwanda, the European Community speeds up its confederation. The Uruguay round of GATT passed and has positioned the stronger nations (Western and others) to take advantage of the unlimited world markets if ratified by the 200 or so participating countries. This means essentially that all the important duties and tariffs will be drastically reduced or eliminated.

This could be especially harmful to Africa which is already a net importer, which means that Africa's stores, marketplaces, shopping centers, and underground economies would be fueled by overseas products without any direct economic benefit to the various nations. A World Bank and Organization for Economic Cooperation and Development study forecasts that the world community (i.e. the West) will be over $200 billion a year richer and that sub-Saharan Africa will be $2.5 billion a year further in debt by the year 2002. Welcome to the new millennium. Seems like we are starting off the next one thousand years like we started off the last.

Few analyses on the world scene are as cogent and clear as those of Noam Chomsky of Massachusetts Institute of Technology. His many books are 'must reading' for a more accurate assessment of the world. A linguist by profession, he stands as the antithesis to such government and private industry mouthpieces as Henry Kissinger. He has been consistent and to the point in refuting the concept of a "free market." According to Chomsky, there is no such animal. He believes that the "leave it to the market" rational has reached myth-like proportions in terms of economic solutions:

> We have to first separate ideology from practice, because to talk about a free market at this point is something of a joke. Outside of ideologies, the academy and the press, no one thinks that capitalism is a viable system, and nobody has thought that for sixty or seventy years—if ever (*The Prosperous Few and the Restless Many*, 9).

However, progressive people should be angered and politicized by what Chomsky reveals about the transnationals:

> Throughout history, the structures of government have tended to coalesce around other forms of power—in modern times, primarily around economic power. So, when you have national economics, you get national states. We now have an international economy and we're moving towards an international state—which means, finally, an international executive.
>
> To quote the business press, we're creating 'a new imperial age' with a 'de facto world government.' It has its own institutions—like the International Monetary Fund IMF) and the World Bank, trading structures like NAFTA and

GATT,...executive meetings like the G-7 [the seven richest industrial countries—the US, Canada, Japan, Germany, Britain, France, and Italy—who meet regularly to discuss economic policy] and the European Community bureaucracy.

As you'd expect, this whole structure of decision making answers basically to the transnational corporations, international banks, etc. It's also an effective blow against democracy. All these structures raise decision making to the executive level, leaving what's called a "democratic deficit"—parliaments and population with less influence.

Not only that, but the general population doesn't know what's happening, and it doesn't even know that it doesn't know. One result is a kind of alienation from institutions. People feel that nothing works for them.

Sure it doesn't. They don't even know what's going on at that remote and secret level of decision making. That's a real success in the long-term task of depriving formal democratic structures of any substance (*The Prosperous Few and the Restless Many*, 7-8).

Dr. Anderson Thompson, historian, political scientist, and one of the great minds of the 20th century argues that the major threat to the development of the African World Community are the two worlds of Europe and Asia. In his article, "The Challenge of the 21st Century: the Establishment of a Grand Center for the African World Community," (Black Books Bulletin, July/August 1991), Professor Thompson suggests that Africa, which in terms of national resources is the richest land on the earth, must prepare for the next century and new millennium by understanding the dangers coming from its traditional enemies, Europe and Asia. His critical eye notes the current difficulties facing Africa: famine, poverty, drought, disease, ignorance, warfare, coup d'etats, small minded leadership, and Western military, cultural, and economic domination. Anderson goes on to state:

Can Africa survive both Europe and Asia? Can we meet the old challenges of our former European slave masters and colonial administrators? Can we defend ourselves against our present Asian merchant-invaders who come bearing newer and even more tempting forms of oppression? Our failure to successfully defeat foreign economic and cultural assaults could mean imminent doom for 30 million African Americans and the entire Black world.

The world is now sharply divided along three distinct and unequal cultural-racial, economic and political lines: Black Africa, the First World; Brown and Yellow Asia, the Second World; and White Europe, the Third World.

The 21st century struggle of the three worlds will be characterized by their antagonistic nationalistic aims. The European world community is presently engaged in a life and death economic war against Asia for world domination of the Atlantic and Pacific Basin communities. Their battle ground is Africa and the rest of the Black world. And while Europe and Asia battle for Africa, the African world seems to lie oblivious, comatose (7).

African Americans (Blacks) in the United States, by and large are not aware of this current onslaught against Africa and its people. The foreign policy of the U.S. is not a topic for conversation as we chomp down our dinners at fast-food restaurants. Randall Robinson, long-time activist and president of TransAfrica (A Black Washington, D.C.-based lobby for the interests of the Black world) has constantly warned us over the years to be mindful of world politics as it affects African people. In April of 1994, he underwent a fast in public protest of the barbaric treatment of Haiti and U.S. policy that refuses Haitians political asylum because of race. He has pointed out that during the years 1980-1990, 76 percent of the Soviet refugees who applied for admission to the U.S. received it compared to 1.8 percent of the 22,940 Haitians who risked their lives on the high seas to get here. Randall Robinson's support and lobbying efforts on behalf of the African majority in South Africa is consistent with his current actions. He cares.

Obviously, Mr. Robinson is not the only African waging this heroic battle to save Africa and its people. However, all of our efforts will simply be pages in books, magazines, and/or newspapers if we do not step up our organization and information distribution. Marvin Cetron and Owen Davies, in their insightful book *Crystal Globe,* define three powerful regional economies that will dominate international commerce. Africa is not a consideration. In the order of their importance they are: European Community (EC); the Pacific Rim-Japan, Taiwan, Singapore, Hong Kong, and Macao, Korea, Australia, New Zealand, and China; and the North American Alliance—U.S. and Canada. According to Cetron and Davies, "vast regions of the earth will be left out of this interlocking arrangement, save on occasions when they can serve the interests of the major powers"(6). Cetron and Davies insist that Africa will remain much as it is now: "little more than stockpiles of raw material, doomed, largely by their own leaders, to poverty and exploitation by the industrialized nations"(6).

That which is consistent in most of the analyses is that the West will continue to run the world. Samuel P. Huntington in his "The Clash of Civilization?" writes:

> The West is now at an extraordinary peak of power in relation to other civilizations. Its superpower opponent has disappeared from the map. Military conflict among Western states is unthinkable, and Western military power is unrivaled. Apart from Japan, the West faces no economic challenge. It dominates international political and security institutions and with Japan international economic institutions. Global political and security issues are effectively settled by a directorate of the United States, Britain and France, world economic issues by a directorate of the United

> States, Germany and Japan, all of which maintain extraordi-
> narily close relations with each other to the exclusion of
> lessor and largely non-Western countries. Decisions made
> at the U.N. Security Council or in the International Mon-
> etary Fund that reflect the interests of the West are presented
> to the world as reflecting the desires of the world commu-
> nity. The very phrase "the world community" has become
> the euphemistically collective noun (replacing "the Free
> World") to give global legitimacy to actions reflecting the
> interests of the United States and other Western powers (39).

The most recent collaboration of the "World Community" was its adventure against Saddam Hussein and Iraq. It cannot be denied that the United States led the West in "liberating" Kuwait for its royal family. The "West" or "World Commu-nity" are also euphemisms for white supremacy. All the nations of the G-7 are white except Japan, who is considered an honorary white country by many political observers.

Lester Thurow strongly suggests in his book *Head to Head* that Europe will come out on top in the 21st century. He writes:

> A case can be made for each of the three contenders [Japan,
> U.S. and Europe]. Momentum is on the side of the Japanese.
> It is difficult to bet against them. The Americans have
> flexibility and an unmatched ability to organize if directly
> challenged. They start out with more wealth and power than
> anyone else. But strategic position is on the side of Europe-
> ans. They are most likely to have the twenty-first century
> named for them...

> Future historians will record that the twenty-first century
> belonged to the House of Europe! (257-258)

What does all this mean to the average person trying desperately to make a living, raise his/her children, and provide for his/her family? Who has the time or interest to be concerned about what is happening around the globe when one's main plan today is to dodge bullets going to and returning from work in many urban areas? Work, jobs, meaningful employment, and who supplies the young with guns and ammunition are all a part of the equation. Civilizations, nation-states, cultures have to be fueled by economics. Money is made in any number of ways: selling one's labor, skills, experience and property, the manufacture and creation of products, farming or agri-business, banking investment, and many others ways. Many men and women study the world primarily to think of new ways to separate people from their money.

However, in the West there has been "perfection" in the area of capital formation and allocation. The West and a few others are not in their dominant economic, political, and military position due to their concern about civilization/culture and others outside of their control. The only way that capital could flow "smoothly" from the poorer nations to the rich one's or vis-versa is that there must be international structures. These structures are known as multinational or transnational companies. These are global companies that according to the United Nations are "associations which possess and control means of production or services outside the country in which they were established." These transnational concerns are profit driven and do not take any prisoners in their fight for market share and world economic dominance.

About twenty years ago, Richard Barnet and Ronald Muller published their *Global Reach: The Power of the Multinational Corporations*, a significant book because it details the rise of multinationals and their impact on the poorer nations and the world. Their model of how executives organize global businesses has become a reality:

> The global corporation is the most powerful human organization yet devised for colonizing the future. By scanning the

entire planet for opportunities, by shifting its resources from industry to industry and country to country, and by keeping its overriding goal simple—worldwide profit maximization—it has become an institution of unique power. The World Managers are the first to have developed a plausible model of the future that is global. They exploit the advantages of mobility while workers and governments are still tied to particular territories. For this reason, the corporate visionaries are far ahead of the rest of the world in making claims on the future. In making business decisions today they are creating a politics for the next generation.

We have shown that because of their size, mobility, and strategy, the global corporations are constantly accelerating their control over the world productive system and are helping to bring about a profound change in the way wealth is produced, distributed, and defended. There are a number of elements in this extraordinary transformation, but the global corporation is the most dynamic agent of change in a new stage in world capitalism (363).

These transnational companies are still the dominant forces on the world's economic playground. The transnational's CEO's and their management with unlimited money, split second communication, and shared values and worldview are now managing the world as they would one of their products: from conception (idea) to production to advertising (marketing) to world distribution to sales. Barnet and Muller name them "the world managers."

According to the *New Internationalist*'s special issue on "The New Globalism" (August 1993), the big players in the 21st century will be the same companies that dominated the last quarter of the 20th century. Of the 20 most profitable transnationals, 13 are U.S. based, 5 are European and 2 are Japanese. The U.K., U.S., France, Germany, and Japan house half of the world's transnational companies and account for about "70% of all foreign investment." Companies like PepsiCo span the globe and employ hundreds of thousands of people with hundred of plants generally producing non-essential products (in the case of PepsiCo, soda pop and other beverages). Of the largest 350 transnationals, their combined sales "exceed the individual gross national products of all Third World Countries." Too often in the Third World—a better description would be misdeveloped world—the local economies are dictated and directed from the outside. The World Bank and International Monetary Fund, both Western creations, play a crucial role in the economies of all Third World Countries. According to the *New Internationalist*, local currencies are often tied to the interest of the transnationals and outside investment "control the fate of nations." Of the 35,000 transnationals, the largest 100 "manufacturing and service companies accounted for 3.1 trillion of world assets in 1990; about 1.2 trillion of that was outside of the multinationals home country." Over seventy percent of world trade is control by transnationals with a small group of companies dominating in the areas of consumer goods, cars/trucks, airlines, aerospace, and electronic components. However, as documented by the *New Internationalist*, the majority of the investments going to the Third World, (about seventy percent) ends up in just ten countries. There is only one African country on the list, Egypt, and there are no sub-Saharan African investments worth mentioning. As the transnationals expand into the Third World, these misdeveloped countries are forced to relax "foreign investment restrictions" thus giving these companies unusual power and influence. And the IMF and WB have forced Third World nations to "sell off state-owned enterprises at bargain-basement prices" as part of "structural adjustment," i.e., rush to

market economies/capitalism. Africa has not been served nor
can it be served by this strategy, nor will the international
institution of GATT help Africa at this time.

In his very important book *In the Absence of the Sacred*,
Jerry Mander gives us a clear picture of why the Utopian
promises of capitalism and technology have not come true.
Mander, also the author of the ground-breaking *Four Arguments for the Elimination of Television*, documents in no
uncertain terms the failure of the policy of unchecked economic
expansion and commodity accumulation. He writes of how
such a policy has brought "social disorder and global environment devastation." His concern is for the "native" peoples of
the planet, primarily in their fight to save their land.

His view is a wide one where the "New World Order" is
being shaped by the most impersonal agenda of telecommuni-
cations, computers, genetic engineering, space exploration,
robotics, and corporate structure. His book is an impassionate
call, better yet demand, for us to challenge what he calls the
mega-technology global world where nature and humans are
irrelevant and subservient to technology, machines, and
transnationals. Mander is an advocate for the planet and the
"native" peoples who still live close to the land and use it in an
ecological way. To him the earth is sacred and a major obstacle
to an ecological and sane future is transnational dominated
corporate culture. He lists what he calls Eleven Inherent Rules
of Corporate Behavior that have allowed transnationals to
dominate the environment and people within it, quoted below
in abbreviated form:

1. **The Profit Imperative**. The ultimate measure of all
   corporate decisions. It takes precedence over commu-

nity well-being, workers health, public health, peace, environmental preservation, or national security....

2. **The Growth Imperative.** It fuels the corporate desire to find and develop scarce resources in obscure parts of the world....the people who inhabit these resource-rich regions are similarly pressured to give up their traditional ways and climb on the wheel of production-consumption....

3. **Competition and Aggression.** Every person in management (is) in fierce competition with each other....This applies to gaining an edge over another company, or over a colleague within the company....

4. **Amorality.** Not being human, not having feelings, corporations do not have morals or activistic goals. So decisions that may be antithetical to community goals or environmental health are made without suffering misgivings....

5. **Hierarchy.** Corporate law requires that corporations be structured into classes of superiors and subordinates within a centralized pyramidal structure: Chairman, directors, CEO, vise presidents, division managers, and so on. The efficiency of this hierarchical form, which also characterizes the military, the government, and most institutions in our society, is rarely questioned.

6. **Quantification, Linearity, and Segmentation.** Corporations require that subjective information be translated into objective form, i.e., numbers. This excludes from the decision-making process all values that do not translate....

7. **Dehumanization.** If the environment and the community are ojectified by corporations, with all decisions measured against public relations or profit standards, so is the employee objectified and dehumanized....

8. **Exploitation.** All corporate profit is obtained by a simple formula: profit equals the difference between the amount paid to an employee and the economic value of the employee's output, and/or the difference between the amount paid for the new materials used in production

(including costs of processing) and ultimate sales price of the processed raw materials....Profit is based on underpayment for labor and raw materials.....

9. **Ephemerality**. Corporations exist beyond time and space. As we have seen, they are legal creations that only exist on paper....

10. **Opposition to Nature**. Corporation themselves, and corporate societies, are intrinsically committed to intervening in, altering, and transforming nature. For corporations engaged in commodity manufacturing, profit comes from transmogrifying raw materials into saleable forms....

11. **Homogenization**. Corporations have a stake in all of us living our lives in a similar manner, achieving our pleasure from things that we buy...all corporations share an identical economic, cultural, and social vision, and seek to accelerate society's (and individual) acceptance of that vision (129-135).

The transnationals move toward "New World Order" is to export homogeneous products, culture, and consumption, making the world's people totally dependent on the product produced by the multinationals. In doing this, they promote a lifestyle of weakening dependency and consumption. As the saying goes, "what's good for GM is good for the world."

Africa

Africa is in serious trouble: economically, politically, and environmentally. Our great historians Cheikh Anta Diop, Chancellor Williams, William Leo Hansberry, John G. Jackson, Edward Wilmot Blyden, Yosef ben Jochannan, John Henrik Clarke, and others have documented the 3000 year onslaught against Africa. The pace for Africa's economic recolonization has not slowed down even though there are a few bright spots on the map. Africa's percentage of the world poor is about 18 percent, but is projected to be 30 percent by the year

2000. In addition to the two-tier attack from Europeans/ Americans and Asians from the outside, one cannot overlook the many internal problems, particularly population growth. With drought, famine, and deforestation threatening Africa's ability to feed itself, it is estimated that Africa's population will double by 2014. Modern Africa started with a stacked deck. Cetron and Davies in *Crystal Globe* put it this way:

> To say the least, Africa has been badly served by its colonial history. The borders drawn by European powers, like those in the Middle East, did not create true nation-states, where people linked by similar ethnic or cultural backgrounds can manage their affairs as a relatively homogeneous group. Instead, they forced native peoples together without regard for tribal identities and animosities. This has permanently scarred African politics (185).

Paul Kennedy in his *Preparing for the Twenty-first Century* gives Africa little chance of success. He points out that the "rising awareness among African intellectuals" and the crys for reform all over Africa, but does not feel that this is enough to change the "attitudes" of African people:

> Population increases, the dimension of grazing lands and food supplies, the burdens of indebtedness, the decay of infrastructures, the reduction of spending upon health care and education, the residual strength of animist religions and traditional belief systems, the powerful hold of corrupt bureaucracies and ethnic loyalties...all those tilt against the relatively few African political leaders, educators, scientists, and economists who perceive the need for changes. As Africa struggles to stay connected with the rest of the world, the inclinations—declining amounts of aid, shrinking trade and investment flows, reduction in media coverage, diminished superpower involvement—are that it is becoming more peripheral. Some experts argue that disengagement by developed countries might have the positive effect of compelling Africans to begin a self-driven recovery, as well as ending the misuse of aid monies. Others feel that Africa cannot live without the West, although its leaders and

> publics will have to abandon existing habits, and develop-
> ment aid must be more intelligently applied. Whichever
> view is correct, the coming decade will be critical for Africa.
> Even a partial recovery would give grounds for hope; on the
> other hand, a second decade of decline, together with a
> further surge in population, would result in catastrophe
> (217-218).

Those of us who have supported, worked for and view Africa as a part of our life-line recognize that economic reform is coming in Ghana, Mozambique, and Zambia. The disman-tling of Apartheid in South Africa is a positive step. If the cease-fire holds in Angola, we will have cause to smile. Namibia and Botswana seem to be reversing their decline. Zaire is still a basket case and will remain so as long as President Mobutu Sese Seko and his corrupt government remains in power. Change is in the wind in Kenya, Nigeria, Botswana, and Tanzania. However, none of this is enough when one reviews the history and struggles against European and Asian encroach-ment that Africa has suffered over the past millennium (see *The Destruction of Black Civilization*). John H. Clarke, in his *Notes on an African World Revolution: Africa at the Crossroads,* chronicles the long, torturous road Africa has had to travel:

> Because Africa is the world's richest continent a great deal
> of the economic strength of the Western world and parts of
> Asia is built on what is taken out of Africa. The continent has
> things that other people want, think they can't do without,
> and don't want to pay for. Africa is the pawn in a world
> power game that the Africans have not learned how to play.
> I emphasized repeatedly that Africa has been under siege for
> more than 3,000 years, and this condition did not change
> with the superficial end of colonialism and an independence
> explosion that had more ceremony than substance. In most
> African countries the condition of the average African
> person has not changed one iota with the coming of "flag"
> independence. All too often Africans fighting for the
> liberation of Africa pronounced to the world what they were

going to do for Africa before they strategically planned how they were going to do it. A case in point is South Africans in the international rhetoric against apartheid. Apartheid is not the main issue in South Africa, bad as it is. If the whites in South Africa eliminated apartheid tomorrow, the Africans would still be in difficulty because they would have no economic power and their land would still be in the hands of foreigners.

Land is the basis of nation. There is no way to build a strong independent nation when most of the land is being controlled by foreigners who also determine the economic status of the nation. Africans need seriously to study their conquerors and their respective temperaments. Neither the Europeans nor the Arabs came to Africa to share power with any African. They both came as guests and stayed as conquerors (384).

Add to this the recent outbreak of AIDS on the continent. The growth of AIDS has the potential to set Africa back even further, if that is possible. This potential catastrophe is spreading like wildfire in central and east Africa. The cause of AIDS is still open to question. Now that the problem exists, how do we stop its spread? AIDS has effectively eliminated the middle generation from millions of families. Cetron and Davis have documented that:

No one yet knows the full impact of HIV on life in Africa, but a few developments are already obvious. Family life has been mutating rapidly under the pressure of the disease. AIDS has cut the middle from many families; grandparents and grandchildren now struggle together to cope with the loss of the intermediate generation. When parents die, other children move in with aunts and uncles. Some families struggle on with older brothers or sisters caring for younger siblings. One study, sponsored by UNICEF, estimates that in ten countries of central and east Africa, up to six million children will lose at least one parent during the 1990s. Most will lose both.

Socially, AIDS is causing the most profound changes since European colonialism. In Zambia, the tradition in some tribes required a man's widow to be purged of his spirit by a cleansing ritual that included having sex with a member of his family. In the age of AIDS, alternative procedures have been adopted. A growing number of people in the tradition-ally polygamous African societies have opted for monogamy. People are marrying earlier to avoid the risk of contracting AIDS in premarital sex. A few even say they will not marry at all unless their potential spouse joins them in an AIDS test (203).

Clearly, AIDS will determine the future allocation Africa's few resources (health, education, medical-care, long-term support). Will this be enough? Again, Cetron and Davies:

And yet even this pales by comparison with the long-term threat facing sub-Saharan Africa. A recent study by the United States Census Bureau and the U.S. Agency for International Development paints a more horrifying picture still. By 2015, the researchers believe, AIDS will kill more than three-fourths of the women who die during their childbearing years, 2.4 million women in that year alone. In some ethnic groups, the disease will kill up to one-third of working-age men. It will cut life expectancy in some cities by nearly twenty years. And it will orphan some sixteen million children. By 2015, the report forecasts, full 17 percent of the African population will be infected by HIV, seventy million people in all (205).

Couple this with ethnic warfare, corrupt leadership, overgrazing and poor agriculture practices, unplanned urbanization (Lagos, Nigeria for example) domestic unrest, overuse of wood and water supplies, territorial and border wars, growing dependency on imported food and medical supplies, lack of long-term investment and poor and insufficient education, political and social structures. For example, serious family planning is almost non-existent in Africa and the education of women is just recently receiving priority in some countries. Africa and Africans must rise to the occasion and change directions if Africa is to survive and develop.

This may sound like an old hat looking for a new head, but education is a large problem in the African (Black) world. We Blacks are truly an international people; we are located all over the globe. However, due to centuries of brain mis-management and mis-education, we do not function as other cultures/races in support-units for each other.

There cannot be harmonious and lasting human development without cultural and scientific education. Education as the cornerstone of culture and remains the engine driving serious people toward genuine human development. In contemporary Africa, a smaller percentage of children receive education than ten years ago. This is a problem all over the Black world. African (Black) people hunger for learning like all people. According to Paul Kennedy,

> Africa has been spending less than $1 each year on research and development per head of population, whereas the U.S. was spending $200 per head. Consequently, African' scientific population has always trailed the rest of the world (216).

He also points out that—in terms of scientists and engineers per million population in the world—Africa is on the bottom, e.g., Japan-3548, U.S.-2685, Europe-1632, Latin America-209, Arab states-202, Asia (minus Japan)-99, Africa-53. African-centered education worldwide is a critical part of the answer to the complex problems facing Africa and its people. It is not too much to demand that our institutions function in the best interest of Black people. However, this will never happen if the leadership views itself as and operates as if it is a part of European or Asian brother/sisterhood. Find your brother and sister within your culture/race first. Complete your own circle before trying to join that of others.

Africans worldwide, but especially in Africa, need an African-centered pedagogy. The European model of education with its Eurocentric hegemonic attitude and practices are still alive and serving the need of Europeans and the few Africans in leadership and power positions. Without a pedagogy that speaks to centering us with a mind that will work against great self-defeating habits/lifestyles we are lost. Everything needs to be re-examined and reconsidered.

1. The role of African women should be at the top of the list. Gender issues, family issues, and the development of children must be given priority. We cannot develop with half of our brain power in bondage.

2. A complete re-evaluation of traditions. Which of our long-standing practices hurt or limit our own development? Is the role of the chief/king still viable in this post-colonial, post-technological world? Why do we not question authority more critically? We must learn to serve and build rather than follow outdated traditional leaders.

3. Should criticism of leadership be at the cost of death, imprisonment, banishment, or ostracism? Are we not allowed to ask questions that are difficult and sometimes embarrassing?

4. What does Pan-Africanism really mean if Africans are not trying to unite Africa into (a) regional economic and military confederations and (b) a "United States of Africa." How does Africa use the talent and resources of Africans outside of Africa. There is some conference sharing going on now. What about more?

5.   We have to stop romanticizing all things African or Black. We contribute to our own misdevelopment when we are not self-critical. All is not well on the homefront (throughout the entire Black world). We have serious economic, political, and "human" problems that will stop any serious development if not addressed. Everything European or Asian is not wrong, and everything African is not right.

6.   Is there one African-centered university in the world? Are there any African institutions of higher education where European, Asian, African, and other modes of development are being studied? We need real research that goes beyond history to an evaluation of economics, politics, and agricultural policies on Africa.

If we continue to give our young people to others to "educate," we will never develop. Over the last 30 years, there have been thousands of African-centered books and materials published that are widely available. In fact the largest association of Black (African) book publishers has been at the forefront of providing African-centered materials. An excellent start for any serious library would be to stock all the titles of member publishers of the National Association of Black Book Publishers (based in Baltimore, MD).

There have been many plans made available to us. We have road maps. The problem is (1) the circulation of them and serious discussion and debate, (2) the belief in the abilities located in the Black world to carry out a world plan for rebuilding, (3) capital and resource formation from the African (Black) world, (4) serious implementation of a world plan, (5) serious assessment and follow-up, and (6) renewing, revising, moving on to the next stage. Where are the African world plans? Study all of Cheikh Anta Diop's work, concentrating on *Black Africa: The Economic and Cultural Basis for a Federated State*, Chancellor Williams's *The Destruction of Black Civilization* and *The Rebirth of African Civilization* and others.

We are not starting from zero. Over the last thirty years, there has been real development in pockets of the Black world. Our task is to make the connections. Join national organizations like the African Heritage Studies Association (AHSA), National Council of Black Studies, National Association for the Advancement of Colored People (NAACP), Association for the Study of Classical African Civilizations (ASCAC), Council of Independent Black Institutions (CIBI), National Black United Front (NBUF), TransAfrica, National Association of Black Psychologist, National Association of Black Social Workers, the thousands of African-centered churches, sororities and fraternities, Sojourner Truth Adolescent Rites Society (STARS), National Black Wholistic Society (NBWS) and others.

Chinua Achebe, in his *The Trouble with Nigeria*, states:

> Patriotism is an emotion of love directed by a critical intelligence. A true patriot will always demand the highest standards of his country and accept nothing but the best for and from his people. He will be outspoken in condemnation of their short-comings without giving way to superiority, despair, and cynicism (15).

Our task is a privilege. We have the rare opportunity to direct, change, inspire, and develop the minds of African people. Our working tools are ideas. The larger question for all of us remains, are we centered in ourselves securely enough to take up battle with the other worlds for the minds of African people?

I close with the challenge issued by Anderson Thompson:

> Guided by the African principle of doing that which serves the interest of the greatest number of African people, we, the Africans in America, can find our rightful place in the African World Community by joining hands with our African brothers and sisters of the Black World in the 21st century search for and establishment of a grand and noble sacred center somewhere on the African continent (8).

References

Achebe, Chinua. *The Trouble With Nigeria* (London: Heinemann), 1983.

Amnesty International Report, 1993.

Ani, Marimba. *Yurugu: An African Centered Critique of European Cultural Thought and Behavior* (Trenton: Africa World Press), 1994.

Barnet, Richard J. and Ronald E. Muller. *Global Reach* (New York: St. Martin's Press), 1991.

Brown, Lester R. et al. *State of the World* (New York: W. W. Norton and Company), 1993.

Cetron, Marvin and Owen Davies. *Crystal Globe* (New York: St. Martin's Press), 1991.

Chomsky, Noam. *Year 501: The Conquest Continues* (Boston: South End Press), 1993.

_____. *The Prosperous Few and the Restless Many* (Berkeley: Odonian Press), 1993.

_____. *What Uncle Sam Really Wants* (Berkeley: Odonian Press), 1992.

Clarke, John Henrik. *Notes For an African World Revolution* (Trenton: Africa World Press), 1991.

Diop, Cheikh Anta. *Black Africa: The Economic and Cultural Basis for a Federated State* (Paris: Presence Africane), 1960.

Kennedy, Paul. *Preparing For the Twenty-First Century* (New York: Random House), 1993.

Kotkin, Joel. *Tribes* (New York: Random House), 1993.

Madhubuti, Haki R. *Black Men: Obsolete Single Dangerous?* (Chicago: Third World Press), 1990.

——————————. *Enemies: The Clash of Races* (Chicago: Third World Press), 1978.

Mander, Jerry. *In the Absence of the Sacred* (San Francisco: Sierra Club Books), 1991.

Said, Edward W. *Culture and Imperialism* (New York: Alfred A. Knopf), 1993.

Thurow, Lester. *Head to Head* (New York: William Morrow and Co., Inc.) 1992.

Wright, Ronald. *Stolen Continents* (New York: Houghton Mifflin Co.) 1992.

Williams, Chancellor. *The Destruction of Black Civilization* (Chicago: Third World Press), 1974.

——————————. *The Rebirth of African Civilization* (Chicago: Third World Press), 1993.

Periodicals

Curtis, Tom. "The Origin of Aids," *Rolling Stone* (March 19, 1972).

Kaplan, Robert D. "The Coming Anarchy," *The Atlantic Monthly* (February 1994), pp. 44-76.

Huntington, Samuel P. "The Clash of Civilization?" *Foreign Affairs* (Summer 1993), pp. 22-49.

Madhubuti, Safisha. "African-Based Education," *Black Books Bulletin* (December 1991), pp. 3-4, 18.

Thompson, Anderson. "The Challenge of the 21st Century," *Black Books Bulletin* (July/August, 1991), pp. 6-7.

The New Internationalist, A Special issue on "The New Globalism," this issue edited by Wayne Ellwood.

Rwanda

Where Tears have no Power

Who has the moral high ground?

Fifteen blocks from the whitehouse
on small corners in northwest, d.c.
boys disguised as men rip each other's hearts out
with weapons made in china. they fight for territory.

across the planet in a land where civilization was born
the boys of d.c. know nothing about their distant relatives
in rwanda. they have never heard of the hutu or tutsi people.
their eyes draw blanks at the mention of kigali, byumba
or butare. all they know are the streets of d.c., and do not
cry at funerals anymore. numbers and frequency have a way
of making murder commonplace and not news
unless it spreads outside of our house, block, territory.

modern massacres are intra-ethnic. bosnia, sri lanka, burundi,
nagorno-karabakh, iraq, laos, angola, liberia, and rwanda are
small foreign names on a map made in europe. when bodies by
the tens of thousands float down a river turning the water the
color of blood, as a quarter of a million people flee barefoot
into tanzania, somehow we notice. we do not smile, we have no
more tears. we hold our thoughts in a deeply muted silence
looking south and thinking that today
nelson mandela seems much larger
than he is.

SUNLIGHT IN THE WEST

THE SPIRIT IN MOST OF US

Religion as Culture

I believe that the religions we practice are not as important as the practice itself. How the knowledge and wisdom gained from one's religion translates into making the world better for all people at a very human and measurable level is what really matters. All "world" religions have moral voices that direct their believers toward that which is good, just, and correct. As a lay-participant-observer, what I have noticed through study, travel, participation, and conversation is that most people have a culturally-based spiritual path in them.

An ethical code is absolutely necessary if we are to have peace and harmony among people. This is not to suggest that such a code of "good" behavior is not attainable in a completely secular culture. Even among the secularist there is to be found a spiritual core that seems to float close to the surface. Such a spiritual core is not necessarily articulated in the literature or language of the "state," but comes through loud and clear in the poetry, fiction, music, dance, visual art, and life-giving actions and artistic creations of most people.

Throughout the vast continent of Africa where hundreds of cultures and languages are practiced, the one connecting thread is that all the people believe in natural powers beyond themselves. Whether one is Yoruba, Akan, Banbara, Dogon,

Ndembu, Lele, Aka, Baka, or Mbuti, there exists a belief system that answers the important questions about life and death. These belief systems (cultures) also guide them in their spiritual and ethical development. As for Blacks in the diaspora, the religious practices are varied and many, with those of Christianity, Islam, and Judaism occupying the minds, hearts and souls of the majority.

That the most self-reliant and visionary of Africans have taken Christianity, Islam, and Judaism and made them "Black" is a profound comment on their desire to be truly liberated. My brief comments here are not to argue for or against any of the world's religions, but to acknowledge their importance and necessity in today's world. However, many religions have been used throughout history to rationalize and justify the activities of slave traders, rapists, serial killers, mass murderers, white supremacists, holocaust makers, capitalists, and "holy men and women" living high on the hog.

Religion is also cultural. Each culture directs, feeds, develops, and disseminates a system of beliefs, values, education, and behavior of its members. That those beliefs, values, education, and behaviors can also be described as a religion indicates how closely culture and religion are interrelated. Annemarie deWaal Malefijt in her seminal study *Religion and Culture* defines religion as culture in this way:

> Religion, like culture itself, consists of systematic patterns of beliefs, values, and behavior, acquired by man as a member of his society. These patterns are systematic because their manifestations are regular in occurrence and expression: they are shared by members of a group. But regularity is not to be confused with homogeneity. In all religions there are differences of interpretation of principles and meanings. There will be found dissenters and believers,

innovators and traditionalists. Dissenters and innovators do not, however, deny regularity: they merely protest against it. When active and successful, they will establish new regularities, to be challenged by others in their turn....

The concepts "cultural" and "social" represent alternative but related ways of looking at the same phenomena. When we characterized ways of looking at religion as "cultural," we saw it as an ordering system of meanings, values, and beliefs by which individuals define their world. These individuals themselves form a society, an aggregate of persons who act and interact on the basis of a given cultural way of life. The specific modes of social interaction based upon religious beliefs give rise to the existence of religious roles and social status and stratification....

Religion is never isolated from other institutions. It has significant influence upon economics, politics, family patterns, technology, and all other important areas of life. This influence is always mutual: these secular institutions, in turn, affect religious forms, values and beliefs. When a society moves from agriculture to industry, its religion will undergo significant changes, but the religious structure itself will also modify and shape the patterns of urban living.

Cultural institutions thus cannot be fully understood if their mutual functions are not taken into account. Religion is particularly important in this respect, because it codifies and expresses the cultural values of the society as a whole. Any functional analysis of religion therefore involves the study of all cultural institutions....

Systems of belief and action involving the supernatural exist in all known human societies. (Some modern societies attempt to repudiate the supernatural, but it is doubtful that they have repressed religion altogether.) The universality or near-universality of religion suggests that it corresponds to otherwise unanswerable questions; it reinforces social values by divine sanctions; it provides hope and consolation (6-11).

If we can agree that religion is cultural, we can also agree that religions are "imperfect" yet always moving toward a "perfection." Likewise, we can agree that each religion has its own path. Often these "paths" clash with one another, producing horrific results, e.g., the Crusades, the Jihads, and the current religious and cultural wars in India, Bosnia, the Sudan, and elsewhere in the world. Of course, these are the dangers of the righteous confronting the righteous.

As a poet of African ancestry, I have given this subject a great deal of thought. Having been raised in a Black Baptist home, with brief visits among the Black Methodists and Catholics, I have come to understand the power, influence, and pull of religion. As I speak around the nation, I am often asked about my religious affiliation. This is a personal matter and I feel little pressure to answer, but, on occasion, especially for young people, I try to accommodate them. My answer is, "I believe in all religions and I do not believe in any of them." As long as one's religion provides life-giving, life-saving, and life-sustaining knowledge and encourages respect for other people and their religion-cultures, I can believe in some aspect of it. However, when a religion proclaims that it is the "only" way, that other religions are "anti-God," and therefore other religions should be banished, then I cannot endorse such a system of beliefs. The major question for me that will not go away is: "Who's religion is right?"

Having traveled widely among many cultures, it would be short-sighted and ignorant of me to even suggest that the Yoruba of Nigeria or the Hindus of India are not "good" religions/cultures and in the same quality "ballpark" as Christianity, Islam, or Judaism. As long as any people's spiritual force answers the basic questions of life, death, future, and how to live a good, just, and quality life, then it is doing its job. In that regard, all religions, perform the same task; there are no inferior or superior religions. They provide answers to the often unanswered questions. They make life livable, understandable, and direct their believers into productive activities.

Religions are moving in the right direction when (1) they serve as enlightening forces to make their believers better, stronger, more understanding, giving, and productive people; (2) when the religions free their believers' minds and allow them to see the world in all of its cultural complexities and inequalities; and (3) when the religions motivate their believers to help the least served among us (regardless of his or her religion).

The spiritual forces that receive the most publicity in the Western Hemisphere are Christianity, Judaism, Islam, Buddhism, and Hinduism. The first three have firm popular support in the United States. Buddhism and Hinduism have strong pockets and are growing. Each of these spiritual/cultural forces are attempting to create moral men and women. And, it seems as though there has been minimal success. However, it must not be forgotten that all of the major Western religions are primarily patriarchal in their control and teachings. Women have, against great odds, made their way in most religion-cultures, but there is still much work to be done in this area. We must be music in each other's ears. We must be water-givers to children as they rise thirsty each morning. We must be strong hands massaging tired backs after a day's work. We must be quiet in the storm. We must be brothers and sisters with long memories. We must be kind and bright smiles to each other. We must listen to our seers and as Howard Thurman insists in his *The Centering Moment*:

> We must remember those who are close to us by ties of blood
> and accommodation, whose needs have been exposed to us

in the days that are behind; those who are sick and who are moving slowly into a terminal dimension of their illness; those who have fallen upon hard and difficult times, from whose hands have been snatched those symbols of security by which the tranquility of their lives have been measured; those who are dependent upon us for things which we cannot give and we do not know how to say we cannot give them. We remember those men and those women whose private lives are burdened by the responsibilities of others and who find, because of the problems which surround them, that their private lives are inadequate and they are lonely and frightened and dismayed. We remember all those who stand within the shadow of the radiance that belongs to the healthy mind and the vigorous spirit; those who are wrestling with inner tortures that pull the world out of balance, who find themselves retreating more deeply within in the hope that in the iron-bound security of their inmost privacy they may be protects from the things that overwhelm and prove unmanageable (36).

The Black Church as an Answer

If we are honest about the social and economic development of African Americans, it is impossible to measure it without taking into account the influence of the Black Church. As tens of thousands of southern Blacks arrived in the cold and hard cities of the North and Midwest, they first found a place to drop their bags and lay their heads. However, when asked where their homes were, they did not give street addresses. Rather, they generally named churches.

The Black Church was the first institution built by the former enslaved Africans after the Civil War. The Black Church was and continues to be family based. The Black Church stands for the values that encourage African Americans to stand on their own two feet. The African Methodist Episcopal Zion Church has a history that dates back to its founding in 1796. It was known as the "Freedom Church" and the bedrock of its faith was the spiritual, social, and economic emancipation of African people. Its early membership included James Varick, Harriet Tubman, Frederick Douglass and Sojourner Truth. Today it has millions of members that spread the globe from Ghana to Michigan, Nigeria to Washington, D.C., India to New York, London to Mississippi, Guyana to North Carolina, Liberia to California. The National Baptist Convention, USA, with a membership of 12 million, is the largest organized body of Black people in the United States. It has churches and members involved in every area of economic, social, and spiritual development that touches the Black community.

If there is to be serious revitalization of the national Black community, it cannot be accomplished without the Black Church. The church is not only aware of this, but is actively taking the lead in many areas. According to Lloyd Gite's cover story of the December 1993 *Black Enterprise*, Black churches in densely populated cities and rural southern states are standing up and reclaiming the leadership in social and economic development.

In cold, hard terms, the Black church is a multi-billion dollar business. The only other Black owned and controlled homegrown Black businesses that can approach the economic strength of the Black church are those involved in the Black hair care/beauty industry and Black funeral homes. However, it is the church with its non-taxed dollars, multi-million membership base, strategic, community based locations and its new highly skilled, university educated leadership that is leading the way to the 21st century.

One of the churches profiled by *Black Enterprise* is the 10,000 member First African Methodist Episcopal (FAME) Church of Los Angeles. To service the rebellion torn community of Los Angeles, FAME created, "the FAME Renaissance Program to fund community services, business and economic development programs through private and public funding sources." FAME Corporation is a nonprofit organization established by the church. They also have the Micro Loan Program, "which supplies low interest rate loans of $2000 to $20,000 to minority entrepreneurs in the area." According to *Black Enterprise*, these type of activities are taking place across the nation as churches under their separately created economic arms expand and grow. They are building senior citizens housing projects, schools, medical clinics, buying and rehabilitating housing and business strips, and funding new business ideas. The Allen Africa Methodist Episcopal Church of New York started financing its many projects out of the collection plate of its 7000 membership. "Today, Allen Church continues to set aside one-third of the $3 million it collects annually." They are major players in the economic life of their community and are currently negotiating with Burger King and Ben and Jerry's ice cream franchises.

The Hartford Memorial Baptist Church of Detroit has led the way in reclaiming their part of that economically depressed city. Detroit, a majority African American city is on its way back after the serious abandonment of whites to the suburbs. Under the enlightened leadership of Reverend Mangedaa Nyathi and Reverend Charles Adams the Hartford Baptist Church is leasing their land to African American entrepreneurs. All across the land, the first institution that Blacks folks built is again capturing the spirit of the 1960s with the "I can, I must, I will" philosophy of leadership.

This is as it should be. It is almost inconceivable to think that we can retake our communities and make them model safe zones and liberated schools for growth and development without the Black church. The memberships of most Black Churches consist of the cream of the Black intelligensia and workforce. If you need attorneys, CPAs, doctors, professors, business owners, construction workers, skilled craftsmen and women, go to the Black church. From the Johnnie Colemans of Chicago to the Calvin Buttses of Harlem to the Michael Harrises of Atlanta to Jaramogi Abebe Ageymans (Bishop Albert Cleage) of Detroit, Atlanta and Houston, to the thousands of ministers of the National Baptist Convention, USA the Black church is again re-establishing itself as the first home of Black folks in America.

Connecting: Self, Earth, Preventive Health

For the last twelve years, I have been working with a group of men who are culturally and politically progressive—The National Black Wholistic Society. We came together primarily because we felt that Black leadership had in their hands more than they could handle on the economic and political front. We felt that we—all over thirty at that time—could provide some leadership in the areas of cultural awareness, self-improvement, self-reliance, and spiritual empowerment.

My own concerns about the inner development of Black people started in 1970. Coming out of the 1960s, immersed in national and international Black politics, I was frightened at my own inability for self-renewal and inner-strength building. By that time, I had become a vegetarian and was deeply involved in the study of alternative health or what is now known as preventive health: the maintaining of the mind, spirit, and body before illness sets in. Dr. Alvenia Fulton, Dick Gregory, Dr.

Roland Sydney and others had led the way in alternative healing in the Chicago area. They provided sound, earth-based, and natural examples of the magical healing powers of the body. They reasoned that this would happen if harmony and balance could be attained and maintained between mind, body, and spirit.

This harmony was possible only if a person could disconnect from the destructive culture surrounding one and actively rebuild from the inside in an environment that enhanced such development. Nature's importance to such a program is now common knowledge. I have written elsewhere about the destructive forces of urban life and the need for the body to be refueled naturally away from concrete, automobiles, skyscrapers, elevators, garbage, human and non-human competition, processed foods, unhealthy water, negative people, negative environments, the rush and hype of the cities, and the absence of clean air, water, plant, and animal life.

Over the last 25 years, there has been an explosion in the alternative health business. Health food stores and restaurants are now located in most highly populated communities. Thousands of books, magazines, quarterlies, and newsletters inform us about the dangers of misusing our bodies and the environment. The President and the Congress of the United States are debating a National Health Plan. People are living longer in the country but most are not healthier. Quality of life is on everyone's lips. However, it is not high on the agenda of many Black folks. Many people of African descent are not taking advantage of all of the new research and new knowledge available to us. There are many reasons for this. The major one is that we are disconnected from ourselves in so many ways.

We must start with the self:
> *little people talk about other people*
> *average people talk about things*
> *intelligent people talk about ideas.*

The perfect idea is in the inner-self of each of us. How do we get there? How do we become larger people?

From Understanding to Knowledge

There are many paragraphs to life. Just as a good reader is able to skillfully maneuver through a book, understand the essence of its content, and grow as a result of his/her reading, each of us must be able to read and feel the many messages in our own bodies and develop preventive measures that will not only maintain our health but prolong and promote wellness. The core of wellness is to understand the preciousness of life and those actions that give and sustain life.

Therefore, life is a balancing of many layers of understanding. The physical understanding is the obvious and most accessible. Our day-to-day decisions are made and acted on here. Our physical consciousness is the loud voice in each of us. This voice guides us every waking moment. However, there is another level of intelligence that many of us never visit. The inner voice, the quiet side, a shared intelligence found in all life, a peacefulness that goes beyond fear and rejection. It is an inner intelligence that does not have a defined limit. It is a stillness that is always there wanting to be activated, to be called upon. It is the intelligence within the intelligence: our spirit or the spiritual self in us. The seeker.

The quality of our lives, and the real beauty in our days is determined by the spirit in each of us and how we share it with

others. We often call this spirit "soul" or "life essence." All
people have it. Most people are unaware of it and therefore do
not use it. Most of us are trapped in the physicality of day-to-
day living. Trying to make ends meet, taking care of children,
finding or maintaining fruitful employment and only allowing
for an emotional release on the holy day of whatever organized
religion we practice. This is positive, but limited and limiting.
We are off center. And much of our confusion is the result of
buying into belief systems that are anti-self. There is a profound
difference between physical seeing and spiritual seeing:

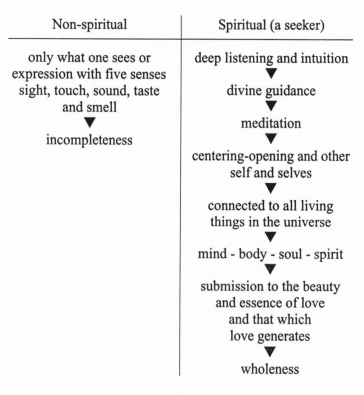

Non-spiritual	Spiritual (a seeker)
only what one sees or expression with five senses sight, touch, sound, taste and smell ▼ incompleteness	deep listening and intuition ▼ divine guidance ▼ meditation ▼ centering-opening and other self and selves ▼ connected to all living things in the universe ▼ mind - body - soul - spirit ▼ submission to the beauty and essence of love and that which love generates ▼ wholeness

(Diagram I)

We must learn to escape or neutralize the fear of fear. Much of our fear is surrounded by death. When we are dead, we are dead. After life is after life. What do we do today to increase the wonders of life for self, family, extended family, and others? We must learn to self-empower ourselves: Only *you* can give yourself the ultimate power needed for transformation. As long as we wait on others, we are running to their time clock and not ours.

One's spirituality is personal. How one chooses to connect to the higher power within us is a personal decision. Often, we need others to tell us that it exists, that there is a profound, loving side of us that we are not experiencing. They too may introduce us to methods of obtaining our inner wisdom. However, it is up to us to nurture the connections. The true spirituality or religiousness of a person has nothing to do with a church, temple, mosque, shrine, or place. It has to do with an attitude, a point of consciousness that accepts the view that there is something greater than one's self at work in the universe. What guides me is my belief that there is a force greater than my physical body. Such a higher power is the source of unlimited energy and goodness and is not depended upon any doctrine, dogma, or person outside of oneself. We must go to the deep self in each of us. This will separate the non-spiritual from the spiritual. (See Diagram II.)

The meaning from within is often distracted by our egos. The answers we seek for a good and productive life are at hand for everyone. However, we must keep in mind that our inner peace must not keep us from joining and being an intricate part of organized efforts to end hunger, child abuse, homelessness, corporate crime, war, white supremacy, poverty, illness, ignorance,

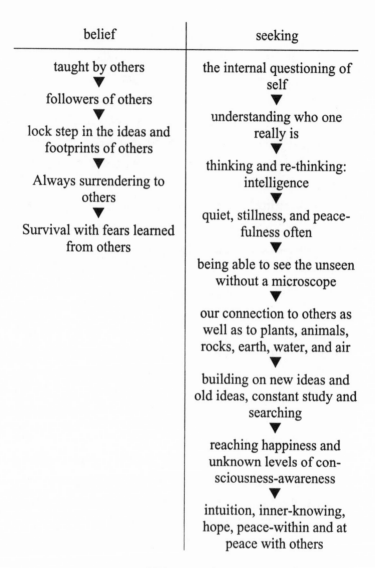

belief	seeking
taught by others ▼	the internal questioning of self ▼
followers of others ▼	understanding who one really is ▼
lock step in the ideas and footprints of others ▼	thinking and re-thinking: intelligence ▼
Always surrendering to others ▼	quiet, stillness, and peace-fulness often ▼
Survival with fears learned from others	being able to see the unseen without a microscope ▼
	our connection to others as well as to plants, animals, rocks, earth, water, and air ▼
	building on new ideas and old ideas, constant study and searching ▼
	reaching happiness and unknown levels of con-sciousness-awareness ▼
	intuition, inner-knowing, hope, peace-within and at peace with others

(Diagram II)

and all the negative aspects of life that allow, encourage, and reward people to be non-productive and inhumane. Our surface knowledge does not allow us to go sub-surface. Surface knowledge seldom gets beyond survival information. If we are to truly develop as whole humans, we must understand the importance of the following:

1. Meditation/prayer, contemplation. Quiet wondering within one's self, breath.
2. Fasting. Inner peace. Cleanliness. Internal cleanliness, inner and physical preventive health. Cleansing and self-healing. Understanding the power of water.
3. Plant life as food (nourishment). Plants are relaxing to be surrounded by and in close proximity to.
4. Relationships (self, family, extended family, others). We are social beings.
5. Exercise. Gathering physical energy, biking, walking, running and active life among nature. Visit parks or natural areas often.
6. Silence. Spirit connections, quietness, slowing down, physically, mentally and internally.
7. Knowledge. Cultural studies, critically questioning one's place in the world, one's own innerself. A continual seeker.
8. Work. Productive actions, creation with hands and mind.
9. Yoga. Quiet reaching. Ultimate relaxing, connecting the physical with the inner.
10. Play. Do those things that bring you peace and joy. Games, inner-attainment.
11. Sex. Physical lovemaking in a reciprocal relationship.
12. Responsible Speaking. Watch your voice. Be careful in your utterances, stay away from lying, gossip, rude speech, and bad language.
13. Responsible Listening. True listening is going outside of

our own egos to hear/feel the words of others with no preconceived notions or prejudices.

14. Rest/Sleep. Our bodies cannot renew themselves without proper rest, peaceful sleep comes when one's life is in a state of findings, when we work and search for the best in all we do.

15. Good manners, kindness and many thank you's for a good life.

All of this is empowering. One cannot talk about self-reliance if one does not start with the self first. Get a hold on your own life and everything else will come together. Unconditional love is not necessarily someone being there for you, but you being there for others and yourself. Is there a higher power? Yes! I experience it each morning as I walk, run, or bike on the lakefront or wooded nature trails. I see it in the billions of different faces, colors, hair grades, smiles, language patterns and approaches to good life that populate this globe. We are one even though many of us are lost, confused, greedy, destructive and enemies to self and the world.

Final Care/Call

This question of health has been a long term concern of mine. All the answers are not in for optimum health. We live in a culture fixated on a diet that is based on the high consumption of meat, fish, and poultry. According to popular culture, the awesome consumption of soda pop, potato chips, candy and ice cream are connected to one's normalcy. If one is not a part of the junk food culture then there is a problem with that person. If one is not sucking on bones at each meal, or stuffing ones self with chemically fed and hormone injected beef and chicken, then one is considered weird or out of the popularity loop.

Preventive health is more than a state of mind. However, it starts there. Eating, over-eating, under-eating, eating poor or good food, eating fast or slow, eating in peaceful surroundings or eating on the run all play an important role in good health. Remember, a waste culture produces a waste mentality. What is more valuable to the maintenance of life? Land, water, oxygen or a new B-2 Bomber at the cost of $ 2.3 billion each?

Can we use common sense as a starting point? If trees are cut down and not replenished in a logical manner, there would soon be fewer trees and fewer animals, insects and micro-organism that depend on the forest. If water is used, wasted, not maintained, cleaned, stored or protected from human and industrial contamination, there would be little water. If top soil is poorly cared for, saturated with the same crop year after year, not allowed to replenish itself, then dust and uncultivated sand results. If the tropical rain forests that provide much of the oxygen, natural healing herbs, and an abundance of wild animal and insect life is removed in the hundreds of acres each day, what happens to the local populations? If human population growth is not slowed (currently about 6.5 billion), or even reversed, will this planet be able to sustain us and continue to renew itself?

Water is more valuable than oil, gold, or diamonds, but is "free" and taken for granted. Fresh water rivers are being used to move the waste of industry, humans, cities, dead water life, and agricultural waste. We have become wanderers ship-wrecked on the ideas of others. That we find ourselves in the back pockets of white supremacists, their supporters, and little men fixated on greed and power who do not care for us, do not respect us or recognize our contribution to world development is only a loud melody in a symphony waiting to be completed. The only answer is for us to become more responsible, caring, and accountable people who are not afraid of power.

We must become a people who do not care what others think about us. The empowering of one's self places the you in you at the center of your universe. As long as we allow others outside of our families or extended families to judge and direct our futures, we will never become centered or focused on that which is best for us or defined by us. Empowerment at its root means being a self-determining and self-reliant person who is secure in one's own personhood and who functions within a knowledge base that is current, cutting edge, and expanding. The ultimate power is to be in control of one's self and to function in a way that such power is multiplied by working with like minded people. We must organize ourselves and our loved ones to fight against the destroyers of life and the earth. Our children will thank us, especially if they are involved in this awesome struggle.

APPROACHING LOVE

Meditation I

There are rumors afloat that love
is ill.
intimacy at best is overnight clashes
and morning regret:
bodies underwashed in strange bathrooms as lovers
& others bang the door softly running.

F ew human acts are as unexplainable as love. Yet most of us
  search incessantly for love while the logic that generated the
journey, with few exceptions, fails to deliver the love we are
expecting. Most people, especially the young, feel that if one
is open to being loved, love will come. However, the when,
how, who, and from what source love enters one's life is always
uncertain. Even how each person defines love is personalized,
complex, and always precarious.

The commonality that personifies love in this culture
varies, but there are three aspects that are generally agreed upon
and crucial: the sharing of quality time, quality space, and
quality connection/communication with a special person. Love
may not start with verbal communication, but love cannot
endure or be confirmed without it. It is also safe to state that if

there is not a quality sharing of hours, special places, and histories, one's heart or spirit may not graduate into the internal spirits of the other.

Language matters. Words used wisely allow a person to enter into another's heart and mind in a unique way. Quality communication is the major connector between potential lovers. Language confirms, respects, or puts on hold possible loveships. Our introduction to the possibilities of love with another person via the language we use is highly cultural and varies in the United States even though we speak a common tongue. Each person is a small river, and his/her voice has its own nuances and variances. Often, when two people of different cultures meet and talk for the first time, one talks "up stream" and the other "down stream." The beautiful possibility is that they are on the same river, trying to get into each other's boats.

Love Indicators

However, before potential love mates get to the language of love, there are several other love indicators that are instrumental. They are sight, smell, touch, spirit/vibrations, style and tones. We see a woman or man whom we have already defined as our type. Such definitions are cultural, racial, often religious and sometimes political and economic. Therefore, there has been a weeding out process that "limits" the pool for us. Men and women have similar but, upon closer examination, different mating strategies.

Visual

The visual selection process is very limiting and often not very accurate or accommodating to long-term needs. Generally, a person's looks hide the deep, deep secrets that often do not allow for or encourage serious love connections. Such secrets represent a person's history, and most Blacks born in the United States have horror stories inside of them. Clearly, such internal histories are stored in the recesses of one's mind only to surface later upon the heels of one crisis or another.

Mature people have learned to read the body language of others. The eyes are especially important in the early stages of a relationship. Many brothers know this and dark glasses are a natural part of their dress. Sunglasses in environments without sun have little to do with protecting the eyes. Being able to read another person's facial expressions from joy to sadness can save one a lot of pain and hurt. Eyes tell the truth.

A person's smiles, frowns, or facial blankness say a lot about the possibilities of love and/or friendship. However, it is in the eyes that one's true self is revealed. There are short stories and poetry in the eyes. The eyes will eventually summon the calm that nurtures a relationship or unleash the storm that checks further development. Early in the sharing or "getting to know each other" stage, the eyes will say yes or no, and sometimes maybe. Occasionally, they clearly state that this is a big mistake.

Smell

Once the visual is confirmed on both sides and the verbal sharing is in process, smell, touch, spirit/vibrations, style, and tones enter the equation. Often the smell of a person in a consumer culture is hidden by the current perfumes of the day. For many people, this is preferable; for others it is acceptable. However, for a growing number, the natural body odor of a potential lover is desirable. Smell is clearly linked to cleanliness, and in this age of sexually transmitted diseases most intelligent people put personal hygiene at the top of their list for likely lovers. The smell of a person is not only obvious in his or her body scent but is quite perceptible in the personal space (home, work, clothing, car, etc.) that one occupies.

do not wait to be loved
seek it,
the unexplainable
fight for love
not knowing whether you have lost or accomplished
poetic possibilities

Touch

To touch or be touched, even in the most casual manner—such as a hand shake or hug—can often define if two people have love possibilities. A person's magic, personality, strength, softness, essence, concern for others and karma are transmitted in the touch. The right touch, the quality of the initial "laying on hands" experienced by couples can suggest many things. Most certainly, the innocence or the complexity of touching, along with the other "love" indicators can clearly prepare a person with a sensitive nature for what is to come or what can come.

Spirit

A largely intangible early love indicator is a person's spirit or vibrations. One often can hear whether or not a person's vibe or spirit is right. Spiritual vibrations are translated in many ways: smiles, laughter, language, mannerisms, the way one eats and the food one eats, clothing, living space, colors, likes and dislikes, personal surroundings (plants, animals, material trappings, etc.); all can enlarge upon a person's spirit or spiritual state. Also, we can tell a great deal about the spiritual nature of a person by the way she or he listens or hears the heartbeat and innerworld of another person.

The highest question, which is not articulated, but is resting—quietly or loudly —in the recesses of one's mind and soul is, "is the *other* person able to feel or sense problems and/ or liberating music in the personhood of a potential lover?"

Connecting spiritually has little to do with religion. The spiritual quality of a relationship speaks mainly to the peaceful-ness, productivity, quietness, reciprocity, shared conscious-ness, creative connectedness, compatibility, energy, and char-acter of the persons involved. Spirit also, and probably most importantly, translates into the trust factor that must be estab-lished early between two people. When the statement is made that "the spirits or vibes are right" between two people, somehow, we know what that means.

A potential lover may fail to interpret another person's spirit accurately because he or she has not learned to read his or her own internal voices and is not at peace with one's self. Such a state can cause one to run elsewhere seeking spiritual qualities in others when one has not taken the time to locate one's own spiritual core, one's own centrality. This is significant because regardless of how a relationship develops, a person will gener-ally spend the greatest amount of time with oneself. Therefore, how a person feels about herself or himself is crucial to the future of extended associations, both personal and profes-sional.

The way a person views herself or himself, her or his level of self-esteem, self-concept, racial and cultural knowledge, personal and professional development and/or advancement, and extended family involvement all contribute significantly to the wellness of a person. By extension, one's active life outside of her or his own "protective" zone depends to a large degree upon the building strengths of her or his zone.

Style

A potential lover's style or manners are extremely important, especially in mature relationships. Personal habits and characteristics that individually mark or identify a person can give an outsider a fuller picture. Whether a person chews gum, picks his or her teeth in public, talks loudly, or the way one wears one's fingernails (not clean or overly painted) are all important in relationship making. The way a person dresses, the facial make-up used, hair arrangement, whether one wears a beard or moustache, or how well it is maintained can be turn-ons or turn-offs.

For many women, even in these days of feminist/womanist liberation (which is sorely needed), good manners are a sign of an intelligent man. For a man to open doors or walk on the outside of the sidewalk, to be mindful of thank-you's when appropriate, to make wise use of telephones, to write notes and letters, and to be considerate of special days in a partner's life contribute greatly to the mating process. Also, being thoughtful and respectful of another person's space and time is a sign of enlightened maturity. For a woman to accept such thoughtfulness from a man is not a sign of weakness, but a sign of security, self-assurance, and knowing that she is valued.

Most intelligent people who are seeking a lovemate are looking for a person who is creative and/or productive. They are seeking a person who is wholistically centered, openly caring, politically and culturally informed, materially and financially "stable," spiritually in tune with the best that the world has to offer or striving for the same. This is why the tone, the quality of quietness and peacefulness generated by two people is of special significance.

Reciprocity

The longevity of a loveship depends largely on how creatively each partner can fit into the unsettled crevices of the other. This means that each person comes to a relationship in formation or already formed, depending on the ages of the partners, and that adjustments (give and take) will occur. In seeking a full life, the understanding and incorporation of the African concept of *reciprocity* is wise to consider. This concept simply states that if a smile is given, a smile is returned; if beauty is offered, beauty is shared; if knowledge is contributed, enlightenment is possible; if one is wrong, the other offers correctives; if one gives 50%, the other partner gives 50% but if one only has 35%, the other partner gladly gives 65% as both work to equalize the giving and the receiving; to give is no less important than to receive. If love is to endure, love is studied, love is shared, love is discovering new days.

Tone

The tone of a relationship is closely tied to the growing environment that two people create with and within each other. It must be happy, but realistic music. Most of us look for people we can grow with. Being able to hear, feel and appropriately respond to the heartfelt needs of the other is a clear sign of reciprocity and longevity. We must learn to play the melody of our partner and do it in a way that is fresh and lively.

Sex

The one aspect of love that is clearly given too much attention is sex, or I should say, sex is not given the right type of attention. Sexual attraction is possibly the most important love indicator for most couples. If two people are only sexually attracted to one another, the odds are that the relationship will be short-lived. Such understanding is critically important for the young, who have not developed fully emotionally and often confuse sexual attraction and/or sexual satisfaction with love. It is imperative to understand that good sex is possible without love. Therefore, every sexual encounter may not be with the person that one truly loves or needs to love.

For example, one partner may be a balloon head and the other a dried-up pea head. A balloon head and a pea head may have a great time in bed for the first six months of their togetherness, but beyond that what do balloon heads and pea heads talk about other than that which is mundane or mediocre? What is created from their union other than baby balloon/pea heads? My point is that two people, if it is written in their minds and hearts and if they are intelligent in their quest, will grow into love, friendship, and sexual fulfillment.

In fact, the ideal state is one where friendship precedes love and sex. If two people can create and actively participate in a working friendship, love—if it is to come at all—will have a better chance of surviving and developing. Often when partners subscribe to the Western "romanticized" concepts of relationships, they end up falling "in love" and just as quickly fall "out of love" at the appearance of a problem unexamined before the sheets were wrinkled.

dig deep for love
search while acknowledging
the complexity of the heart & fading standards.
in seeking love use care
to let strangers into you
too quickly
may make you a stranger to yourself.

Most people do not grow up with "good" sex education. Sex for the young is often foreign and frustrating. Generally, sex comes after a long line of well-played rituals: meet and talk, a date and maybe a light kiss, more meetings and conversation generally in a neutral location. Around the second or third week, another date—which may include dinner and a movie. The conversation is toward finding common ground. By this time, the young man would have met the young woman's parents. Sex is discussed between them, kissing is more passionate and probably heavy petting is taking place. A part of the ritual is getting to know one another and the establishment of "feelings" between the two people. Sex should not be the start of a relationship; sex is something beautiful and sensitive to look forward to. A part of the search is in the mystery and is in the find. There is always the investment of time into one another. For a woman to sleep with a man was/ is a serious decision. In my youth having sex made a statement about how a woman felt about a man. Most of all, it was a commitment of feeling and caring. Most would call it love. Sex, more often than not, was a carefully defined commitment to a person. Generally, marriage or a long-term bond or binding relationship followed.

Too many young people are being introduced to sex too early and incorrectly. In urban communities, the major sex educators are the street and mass media—with television taking the lead in defining "acceptable" parameters. By and large, street culture and mass media (especially since the advent of cable television) portray women as mindless vaginas using their sex and sexuality to sell meaningless materialism. Among too many urban young males, the references attached to women, specifically Black women, are insulting and debilitating. Terms like "bitch," "ho," "cunt," and "nigger woman" are used with little thought or understanding of the damage they do and the extent to which they reveal the user's acceptance of a white supremacist commercial culture that devalues all women.

This profound level of disrespect for women in Western culture is not new, nor is it the result of the influence of electronic media or the woman's movement. The degradation and control of women have their foundation in a racist, material-based, patriarchal and sexist culture. In all aspects of this society—from religion to law, education to miliary, the arts to finance—women are at best tolerated and patronized. Much of their advancement is indeed based on merit.

Friendship to Loveship

The friendship route to love is not to be taken lightly. In many ways it has replaced courting, which some view as old-fashioned, but which served mainly as a safety valve to get to know another person. Beginning with friendships can prevent one night stands that can be dangerous and deadly. The necessity of knowing a person speaks loudly to the quality of the knowers. One must protect the psychological core of one's personhood. Opening oneself up too quickly to emotional sharing, material dependency, or sex can be most profound in determining success or failure in a relationship.

Walking into a loveship rather than running into sex is essential for lasting love. Men must learn that most women would rather wait for sex and not be pressured early into a sexual relationship. Most intelligent women want to be wanted (needed) for more than their ability to sexually stimulate and satisfy a man. In fact, sex or love-making is less than 20% of a serious loveship. Most partners' sharing is "nonsexual." This is why productive and creative minds are essential to quality loveships.

Most of us, no matter how experienced, come to new love as novices. Newness brings unknowns and complexities especially at the sexual levels. Each new person is like a giant jigsaw puzzle or a large forest with many streams, much vegetation and wildlife. We are as different as the billions of faces that populate this magnificent planet. Few of us have been taught—really schooled properly—to be lovers. Too often, we learn on the run or in the search for "fun."

Sometimes this works; most of the time it does not. Thus, millions of marriages and relationships fail in the United States each year. If love, which incorporates healthy and loving sex, is to have meaning and longevity in one's life, deep understanding is necessary. To reach such an understanding requires serious and ongoing study, cooperative "practice," and contemplation. It requires loving whispers, eye-to-eye speech, as well as before, during, and after play that is sensitive to one's partner's needs.

The commercialization of sex has demeaned its value and placed it in the back alleys of many men's minds. The *Playboy* and *Penthouse* mentality among many men, and growing numbers of women, is the norm rather than the exception. There are few aspects of life that are as satisfying and beautiful as two lovers enjoying the gifts of each other. Part of the beauty is in the search, in the finding, in the small but enlightening discoveries that help to blossom a loveship. The fitting into each other in those natural places reserved for the most intimate and sensitive of meetings is the introduction that millions of people never fully experience.

Beauty

The one area that I purposely saved for last is that of physical beauty. We each define what is beautiful in our own minds. The only advice I would give is that the more "beautiful" a person is the deeper her or his secrets are in this culture. This is due primarily to the commercialization of beauty. The exploitation of physical beauty is a multi-billion-dollar business that takes no prisoners. Physical beauty is not just for the young. One can preserve one's attractiveness into the elder years. Stay in shape, eat properly, exercise, study health and try to function in an enlightened extended family community that is not afraid to stay in shape, mentally and physically.

There is so much that can be written on this subject. It is best that I end as I began: speaking about the possibilities. Listen to your heart, but don't lose your head. Try to travel in order to experience other cultures, ideas, and spirits. Stay close to nature and that which is natural. Don't be fooled by the weakening limitations of false food, false gods, false people, false ideas, or false love. Walk into love, grow into love, never give up on the search, and remember to smile often in your travels.

from dawn to dusk in cities
that sunrises often fail to visit
we imprisoned light & generated heat.
you are seedless grapes and
bright stars at winter & wind,
there are voices in your smiles
and confirmation in the parting of your lips,
you speak in laughter and pain,
are vibrant woman approaching dreams
knowing disappointments,
accepting quality.

MAINTAINING LOVESHIPS

Meditation II

L ove is a living river running slowly north to south, travers-
ing the entire human continent. Love is like the Mississippi
River experiencing all types of weather, hot to cold, warm to
cool, frigid to steaming hot. Find the weather of the person you
love; monitor it often as you learn to swim upstream together.
However, remember that love is not a swimming contest, and
most of us will never learn to backstroke. There are many
paragraphs in a life of love. I say "paragraph" because the
stanza of poetry is still foreign to most of us.

Bonding, mating, and preferably marriage to another
person is or can be music. Much of the time, in this culture, it
is regrettable noise. However, it can be the best of the early
Supremes, Miracles, Four Tops and Nat King Cole. Some of
us measured our early happiness with each new cut by the Dells,
Stay in My Corner. Coupling is also Bessie Smith, Billie
Holiday and, yes, Nina Simone—as they sing with tears in their
eyes, *Am I Blue*? We choose our dancing partners. We can
either two-step, tap, do modern, African, the breakdown, or get
in line and pulse. Or like the river's weather, we can adjust our
body temperatures to accommodate the other in our lives and
adapt to our own definitions of happiness, stability, and seriousness. Whatever tune we choose will demand work, require

navigating the personal river of the other, require the sharing of the most intimate spaces. We may be southern in our spirit, yet, too often our struggle is to neutralize the northern winds blowing ice into our lives. Think in bright possibilities.

To the Men

Women are different in so many beautiful ways. I wonder if we men really ever sit down within our own questions and ponder the complicated melodies of the woman/women in our lives? Do we ever try to put our feet and souls into their shoes and spirits? Each woman is her own color, is her own stream, is her own season, and has her own personal weather report. We must listen to the wind of our women. Often it comes with hurricane force, but mostly it arrives smoothly so as not to take either of us off center. The women in our lives are the balances that keep our families from falling too far off course. If there is to be "war," let it be against superficial assessments of women. Do not fear intelligent, self-reliant, independent, strong-willed, and culturally focused women. Seek them. Most of these women have strong backs and deep wells. They harbor ships of love. They also hold within them the pain and happiness of large families and culturally defined histories. The most serious of them think in long distances. If they are with children, they function always with a clock in them. They carry the pulse of their children close to their hearts. They also carry the smiles of the men they love tightly in the vicinity of the same heart.

To the Women

Men are beautiful in so many different ways. They come with unorganized heartbeats. They come, often ready to learn, ready to be taught a different rhythm. Like their toes, the size and shape of their hearts are hidden complicated fears. Young men fear women. They hide their fears in muted language and quiet cool. At dances, they hold up walls with their backs, a mean lean carefully shaped to give off messages of "I'm ready." Generally with one or more of the brothers they signal that, "We're ready." "Ready for what?" is the question. Too many men function overtime in ways to impress other men, mainly their fathers or mentors, brothers, uncles, grandfathers, teachers, or coaches. We buy into the "impressions" business too early. Often the men talk in codes. We do not talk or sing to the woman/women in our lives the music that is pulsating in our minds. We do not beat around the bush, we beat the bush. We think that we are lovers, or we want to be lovers, but seldom contemplate the meaning of love. Many of us have been taught "love" by our peers and the street. Too often this is translated into the physical only. Men need understanding, good instructions, and magic in their lives. Women represent all of this to us. But we do not listen. Women also represent children, commitment, sharing, and long-distance conversations about tomorrows and fears. Too many men come ill-prepared for love, for sharing, for deep-river rides, having spent too much time in the northern hemisphere of their minds. We must begin to carry the spirits of our women in us, to open our mind's eye to the great possibilities that serious mating represents for our future.

Marriage is not a vacation or a prolonged holiday. Eighty percent of a marriage is work, compromise, adaptations, changes, intimate conversations, laughter, sexual sharing, confusion, joy, smiles, tears, pain, crises, re-education, community, apologies, mistakes, more mistakes, new knowledge, and love. If children are involved, include parenting and repeat everything above twice for each year of the marriage. If the marriage lasts more than fifteen years, the couple should add wisdom. What about the other twenty percent? I presume that even in the most successful of marriages, the couple will sleep.

Remember, the deepest hurt is the hurt inflicted by lovers. To remain lovers is hard work; it is not natural. Mating/ marriage is cultural. Most things grow old. The key to beautiful tomorrows is involvement in a loveship that ages gracefully. We are bound to make mistakes in our loveships, but the lesson is to learn and grow from them. Always listen to your mistakes.

If Black women do not love, there is no love. As the women go, so go the people. Stopping the woman stops the future. If Black women do not love, strength disconnects, families sicken, growth is questionable, and there are few reasons to conquer ideas or foes. If Black men do not love, shouting starts, the shooting commences, boys fill prisons, and our women grow gardens off to themselves. If Black women and men love, so come flowers from sun, rainbows at dusk. As Black women and men connect, the earth expands, minds open and our yeses become natural as we seek

quality in the searching,
quality in the findings
quality in the responses
quality in the giving and the receiving,
quality in love,
beginning anew,
always and always
fresh.

PARTING LOVERS, A CLOSING WITH RENEWING POSSIBILITIES

Meditation III

Part I.

There is more in the missing and the giving than in the receiving. When love leaves, melody leaves, songs cease, laughter becomes measured and brightens one's face less often. Touch or being touched becomes highly discriminatory. Certain touches are avoided. When love leaves, a tearing takes place; it's like the center of one's heart being ripped apart and exposed unfiltered to sand or acid, like pollution. Sleeplessness follows, one's inability to eat, and the sudden loss of weight is inevitable for many. Others put on weight. The gaining of weight impacts the body; "junk food" and guilt takes the place of internal cleansing. When love is missing or detained, there is a constant hit in the pit of the stomach, simulating an indefinable emptiness. The loss of love is the losing of a precious part, like being lost in action, the missing other in you. For serious lovers, for contemplative lovers, for lovers who understand the silk-like concentration of energy and spirit required, it will take the noise and force of hurricanes, the lava of volcanoes, and the disconnectedness of earthquakes to confirm the undoings of this loveship. The quieting of this kind of love is not an often occurrence, once in a generation, maybe twice in a life-time. Such love is heart-rooted, sexually measured (hot), thoughtfully shared, consistent, a slow and deliberate love which will take the cultures and breathless thoughts of loving others to demand its transition.

Part II.

Where end to end becomes beginning to beginning. The releasing of mind, soul, and spirit. The best cure for transitional love is to leave lovingly. To refocus and communicate, digest and internalize the crackings and earth-movings in your hearts. The ultimate healers for parting lovers is rest, is meditation, is re-evaluation of one's loveship. Healing requires waiting time, demands thinking time, needs liberating and insightful music. Healing could be a sharing of pain with a trusted friend—a talking it out. More waiting time. Avoiding blame. Reconstructing of beautiful memories. Rebuilding thoughts. Conversations with one's self. Meditation. Deep study and creative production. Exercise. Fasting. Cleansing. Cultural inner attainment. Meditation. Surrounding one's self with nature and music, art literature, dance; the quiet beat and rhythm of new life. Searching softly for the simple rejuvenative powers of nature. Reach for colors that are reflective. Search actively for certainty, smiles, and learned exactness of blooming new love. Take your time in the searching. Rising in this vast world are renewal possibilities. Spring, at planting time. New heat coming. Soon.

Part III.

If parting is necessary
Part as lovers.
Part as two people
who can still
smile & talk & share
the good & important
with each other.
Part
wishing each other
happy
happy life
in a world
fighting against the
men and the women,
sisters and brothers
Black as
we.

SANKOFA

Film as Cultural Memory

Haile Gerima, the award-winning Ethiopian film maker and Howard University professor, has always been a serious man. He knows America like he was born here. His double heritage, African and African living in America (he has lived and worked here twenty-five years), has prepared him to create a film of a life time. *Sankofa*, his new film about the enslavement of Africans and the psychological and violent liberation of a few of them, is a first in Western filmmaking. It is a riveting examination of a piece of history that is enormously powerful and prophetic in its telling of our story.

Gerima, as the brothers and sisters would say, "has been around the block." He has been making films for over twenty years. I first met him in the early seventies when I also taught at Howard University. His earlier films—*Bush Mama, Child of Resistance, Harvest 3000 Years*, and *Ashes and Embers*—have led the way in Pan-African/Black liberation filmmaking. His body of work demonstrates that he is not only consistent in theme, historical accuracy and political point of view, but that he is a visionary and an artist. As visionary, he must take chances; he must explore the world from his insides. As an artist, he not only crafts a film in the intricacy of his profession, but goes sub-surface looking for meaning, looking for the story within the story, not settling for the easy questions or answers. His work has always made us uncomfortable in our post-enslavement existence.

Sankofa, from the Akan proverb, *se wo were fi na wo sankofa a yenkyi* (it is not forbidden to go back and claim what you've forgotten) is a spiritual film of memory and resistance. This is an African (Black) narrative that starts in the present on the coast of Ghana, which was known as the Gold Coast prior to the presidency of Kwame Nkrumah. *Sankofa* travels through the eyes of Mona/Shola (Oyafunmike Ogunlano), a high fashion model who dances to the lusty camera of a white photographer. The photographic shoot takes place on the grounds of Cape Coast Castles—the launching point of millions of African souls across the Atlantic into enslavement. Sankofa, the divine drummer and rememberer (griot), constantly interrupts the photographic shoot as well as the tours that takes place at the Castles. Sankofa, played by the musician/elder, Kofi Ghanaba, represents memory, pain, protector of hollowed grounds, and African strength. In his confrontation with Mona, he strongly demands that she return to the source and rediscovers her true self.

Mona, in a blonde wig and mini skirted, body displaying outfit is the best example of a Negro, a sorry white invention, who hates herself and who has lost history only to be re-enslaved into a twentieth-century lifestyle that is embarrassing and degrading. The opening scenes are drum-filled with ancestral chants of "spirit of the dead rise up and claim your story." As Mona, on the urging of Sankofa, investigates the slave dungeons, she is literally kidnapped into her past. She is captured, stripped of her modern identity, profession, and memory, chained and taken back to an American plantation and reappears as a house slave named Shola.

This is where Gerima, writer, director, editor, and co-producer becomes filmmaker and story teller. He moves slowly and deliberately in introducing us to the film's characters. His is a studied style, reminding one of the novels of Ayi Kwei Armah (*Two Thousand Seasons* and *The Healers*), the liberating historical works of Chancellor Williams (*The Destruction of Black Civilization*) and John Henrik Clarke (*Notes on an African World Revolution*). In filmmaking, he is in the tradition of Ousmane Sembene, Med Hondo, Flora Gomes, and others. *Sankofa* is a story of oppression, but is not oppressive in its telling. It is an African-Black point of view that shames the tradition of *Mandingo*, *Superfly*, *Uncle Tom's Cabin*, and all the Black exploitation films of the 1960s-1980s.

We meet the rebellious and uncontrollable field slave Shango (Mutabaruka). There is the equally strong and insightful queen-mother Nunu (Alexandra Duah) and her half-white, self-hating son Joe (Nick Medley), a house slave captured by the enormous pull of Christianity and a white lifestyle. In fact, Christianity in the presence of a white, Catholic priest, Father Raphael (Reginald Carter) is the undying contradiction and "centering" conflict that haunts Joe and Shola, especially in her non-violent feelings that she fights throughout the film.

Sankofa, without apology or self-indulging, details the African side of enslavement in all of its inhumanity and brutality. This is not a Hollywood film. It took Gerima twenty years, with a budget of about one million dollars. As I write this essay, the film has not been picked up by a major distributor. Therefore, Haile Gerima has had to add to his credentials that of distributor. Why? Because *Sankofa* is not a victim-oppressive re-telling of how Lincoln freed the salves. It is not a retelling of how the white "master" was really a good man at heart, but caught up in the economic, political, and historical forces of his time and had few choices if he was to live well and in a privileged way. This is the first film I have ever viewed where there are no good white folks involved in the trading of African people. That in itself is progressive. It is simply naive at best and down right ignorant at worst to think that the horrible institution of slavery could have existed so long if there was not common agreement and compliancy among the majority of white people involved in it. Gerima's retelling of the African holocaust is not a sanitized version of suffering Negroes, but is a culturally focused, politically clear, non-romantic introduction to the strength, complexity, culture, humanity of enslaved African people. Gerima clearly presents the complexity of an institution that was organized to break the will and spirit of those it enslaved, while reaping the slaveowners and slave traders huge profits and power. He also depicts the genius with which the same institution simultaneously made enslaved Africans enemies to themselves. It reminds me of the words of the great poet Leon Damas warning us to be aware of the "plantation mentality, whether you are a plantation owner, plantation master, or plantation slave." *Sankofa* evokes such memories and makes it a film for today.

Throughout Western film history, there has always been the white point of view. There also exists the Negro slave point of view—which is actually white-colored Black. Now, in Sankofa, we have an African-Black point of view. This departure is powerful and believable in its articulations that

African people are much more than what one sees. Gerima's use of narrative, flash backs, mythologies, non-linear story line, nature, poetry and African music—with the African drum as central as a heartbeat—puts him in the company of great filmmakers. Just as important, he does not fail us by lying or covering up our own weaknesses and complicity. He is a brave and culturally conscious African (Black) film maker who obviously loves his people. This love, this uninhibited attachment, (we call it family) is the spirit that moves and motivates this non-traditional masterpiece.

Sankofa makes us think. It brings water to our eyes. It forces us to reconsider our lives and those we love, live, work, and play with. It is a reflective mirror that positions us in a context and content which is not debilitating to our psyche, not a stop-sign to our future, but is revelation. It is a spiritual work of multiple possibilities that skillfully introduces a new film language. To most of us, such a language is foreign to our experience. This is a Pan-African-Black film of determination, insight, and liberating encouragement. Gerima sets a new standard of advocacy filmmaking. He takes a position.

Gerima's perspective is a learned, experienced, and in-spired one. Few could have made such an insightful film. He is in his element and like the recently published *Yurugu: An African Centered Critique of European Cultural Thought and Behavior,* by Marimba Ani, *Sankofa* will not receive the audience it deserves unless we help. One of the major indica-tions of our powerlessness is the lack of Black film theaters owned by African Americans. In the entire nation, Black folks own less than five. For a population of forty million plus, whose major entertainment outlet outside of television is movie-going, this is embarrassing and pitiful. For a people whose gross national product is over $350 billion, this is inexcusable. After twenty five years of Black exploitation films which generated billions of dollars in profit, all Blacks have to show for the films' existence is the new life they are given at video rental outlets.

In *Sankofa,* the question of empowerment and of land ownership continues to speak to the condition of African (Black) people. It goes something like this: Europeans (whites) stole and colonized the Americas, committed genocide (Holocaust) against the indigenous peoples (in excess of forty million killed), and gained control of this vast continent and its untold riches. Europeans needed workers—indentured whites were not enough and the indigenous people continued to fight and die rather than work their land for others. Their next option, take the Africans from their land (African Holocaust), which was also being stolen by Europeans (whites), to work in the Americas for Europeans. The underlying message of *Sankofa* is that all life starts with the care, use, exploration, repair, fertilization, maintaining, and love of people and land. If you destroy the land, the destruction of its people will follow. Welcome to Black (African) USA 1994. We are a landless people, begging the people who created our condition for jobs and a theatre to show an African-centered film.

Sankofa is a film of bright but horrible memory. *Sankofa* is Haile Gerima's liberating message in a medium which ninety-eight percent of our people watch and support. He is not alone in his understandings and messages. Many have preceded him. Because of his work, many others will follow. *Sankofa* warns and prepares the listeners and viewers in a way that our best poets and fiction writers have been doing for generations. *Sankofa* is a spiritual and violent film. However, the violence is primarily off screen, while the spiritual nature of African people is highlighted and provides the core linkage between Blacks worldwide. Who among the culturally conscious can forget the urgent words of Ayi Kwei Armah's *Two Thousand Seasons*:

> The linking of those gone, ourselves here, those coming; our continuation, our flowing, not along any meretricious channel, but along our living way, the way: it is that remembrance that calls us. The eyes of seers should range far into purposes. The ears of hearers should listen far towards origins. The utterer's voices should make knowledge of the way, of heard sounds and visions seen, the voices of the utterers should make this knowledge inevitable, impossible to lose.

> A people losing sight of origins are dead. A people deaf to purposes are lost. Under fertile rain, in scorching sunshine there is no difference: their bodies are mere corpses, awaiting final burial.

Sankofa can be a wake-up call for sensitive viewers, listeners, and remembers. We, African people, Black diaspora people, are a part of this world too. Are we destined to be job seekers in the ideas and models of other people's worldviews? Haile Gerima has given us both questions and answers. As the brothers and sisters say, the ball is in our court. Will we learn their game or create new ones? It is not forbidden to go back and claim what you've forgotten: *Sankofa*. Can we build on that lesson?

GWENDOLYN BROOKS

Distinctive and Proud at 77

how do we greet significant people among us,
what is the area code that glues them to us,
who lights the sun burning in their hearts,
where stands their truths in these days of MTV
and ethnic cleansing,
what language is the language of Blacks?

she has a map in her. she always returns home. we are not
open prairie, we are rural concrete written out of history. she
reminds us of what we can become, not political correctness
or social commentators and not excuse makers for Big people.
always a credit-giver for ideas originated in the quiet of her
many contemplations. a big thinker is she. sleeps with paper
and dictionary by her bed, sleeps with children in her head.
her first and second drafts are pen on paper. her husband
thinks he underestimates her. she thinks we all have possibili-
ties. nothing is simplified or simply given. she wears her love
in her language. if you do not listen, you will miss her secrets.
we do not occupy the margins of her heart, we are the blood,
soul, Black richness, spirit, and water-source pumping the
music she speaks. uncluttered by people worship, she lives
always on the edge of significant discovery. her instruction is
"rise to the occasion," her religion is "kindness," her work
is sharing and making words matter. she gives to the people

everybody takes from.
she is grounded-seeker. cultured-boned.
she is Black sunset and at 77 is no amateur.
rooted willingly and firmly in dark soil, she is last of the great
oaks.
name her poet.
as it does us, her language needs to blanket the earth.

BEGINNINGS AND FINDINGS

Conclusion

I refuse to fall into the mindset of thinking that I am "right" all the time. It is too much of a burden and an illusion for one's ego to think that one cannot be wrong about many things in life. The first trap of the pseudo-intellectual is to have the answers for all questions.

I've lived long enough, studied deep enough, traveled far and wide enough, and experienced failure, success, disappointment, joy, foolishness, ignorance, love, stupidity, and hatred often enough to understand that my interpretation of "reality," as "fact" and the "truth" are not always correct. This is also to acknowledge that I will not knowingly write or speak a falsehood. Due to my Western orientation and limited education, I have experienced brain mis-management like most writers and thinkers in the West. As a poet and writer, I will always be a student. As a student, I will always seek to improve.

It is somewhat liberating to realize that I do not have the answers to most of the difficult and not-so-difficult questions in the world. This understanding only makes me more careful as I seek enlightened levels of knowing. It is also liberating to observe the creations of others without constantly comparing my own output/production to theirs. Small mindedness by definition devalues the contribution of peers. Sorry, let me correct myself: small mindedness dictates that one does not have any peers. Therefore, one does not acknowledge the contribution of others.

I was asked once if I preferred a room full of men and women who have read, understood, and championed my work without question, or a room full of critics that found true philosophical differences with some of my conclusions and constantly challenged me on them. I picked the latter primarily because I have seen the danger of "rah-rah" crowds and I have noticed how their presence stops intellectual development, quality research, thinking, and writing.

A part of the poet/writer's responsibility is to facilitate and encourage deep thought. For too many people knowledge and education are like potato chips, eaten often to ease one's hunger but not substantive enough to facilitate real growth, insight or prolong health. And, like potato chips, there are literally hundreds of competing brands—each representing a minor variation on a theme or taste to capture a greatly diminished thinking population.

We now have in our community a significant Black middle class who for the most part is a self-hating miserable lot, lost in Eurocentric ignorance and living with the illusion that they can somehow buy themselves into whiteness on a bi-weekly pay-check. That such a actions only further imprisons them in the web of consumer conduct escapes most of them despite their credit card filled pockets.

This class, for the most part, will stand in line to but the latest toys produced in the U.S., Germany, France, England, or Japan as long as the directions for their use are not too complicated or wordy. It never enters their minds that the key to true happiness and worthiness is to be a creative producer of needed goods and services for others. They do not understand that in a capitalist society one must learn early how to say NO! No to foolishness, no to self-hatred, no to trying to keep up with people who do not like you, and no to the many wishes of our children that a material culture cultivates.

The children of this new Black middle class are often a selfish, ego-consumed, self-centered, and self-hating group which has been taught that the world revolves around them. Even though many of them attend the nation's best colleges and universities, they are at best mediocre students who feel the world owes them something. That something is mainly defined as material. Many of them are truly spoiled, only respect money or pleasure, and—if they do not self-destruct—may end up being our leaders tomorrow.

We are living in a time of deep fragmentation and disconnectedness. A part of the problem is identification. Confirmation of identity is necessary, early and often for our children. Yes, we are people of African descent. We populate much of the world. We are more than branches of a deep-rooted tree from Africa. We are African (Black)-rooted wherever we are. We must be powerful because everybody on the earth *reacts* to us. How does one harness such power and direct it positively? That is what this book has been about:

a call to serve rather than take,

a call to help rather than reject,

a call to save rather than buy,

a call to conserve rather than shop,

a call to contribute rather than consume,

a call to produce rather than beg,

a call to build rather than destroy,

a call to create rather than marvel in other's creations,

a call to study rather than stand by and watch,

a call to love rather than hate,

a call to return to the center in you.

■

———————— *About the Author* ————————

An advocate of independent Black institutions, Haki R. Madhubuti is the founder, publisher and editor of Third World Press, founder and current board member of the Institute of Positive Education/New Concept Development Center, president of the African American Book Center, publisher/editor of *Black Books Bulletin: Words Work* and professor of English and director of the Gwendolyn Brooks Center at Chicago State University. He is a founding member of the National Black Wholistic Retreat Society and the Organization of Black American Culture. In 1990, he served on the National Commission on Crime and Justice.

Madhubuti received the African Heritage Studies Association's Community Service Award (1994), the American Book Award in 1991, and was named Author of the Year for the State of Illinois by the Illinois Association of Teachers of English (1991). He has been poet-in-residence at Cornell University, Howard University, and Central State University. He is an active lecturer, community worker, and researcher in the area of culture.

He is the author of 19 books, emerged on the literary scene in 1967 with the widely read *Think Black* and *Black Pride* (1968), and became recognized as one of the critical Black poets of the Sixties with the 1969 publication of *Don't Cry, Scream*. Haki Madhubuti's most recently published work, *Black Men: Obsolete, Single, Dangerous?* has sold in excess of 200,000 copies. His work has been highlighted on CBS's *Nightwatch*, National Public Radio's *All Things Considered*, the *Washington Post*, the *New York Times*, the *Chicago Tribune*, *Essence* magazine, *Black Entertainment Television*, *The MacNeil/Lehrer News Hour*, and the *Chicago Sun-Times*. He lives in Chicago with his wife and children.